CONVERSATIONS WITH OLIVIER MESSIAEN

Claude Samuel

translated by

Felix Aprahamian

STAINER & BELL
LONDON

Original (French) edition:
© 1967 Editions Pierre Belfond

English edition:
© 1976 Stainer & Bell Ltd
82 High Road
London N2 9PW

SBN 85249 308 8

Printed in Great Britain by Galliard (Printers) Ltd,
Great Yarmouth

Conversation 1

CLAUDE SAMUEL. Olivier Messiaen, facing you with a brief to
question you, I am perplexed; your work is so rich, so prolific,
and your personality so reticent and so winning that I don't
know how to tackle them. My first question, then, concerns the
basic reasons of your work as a composer. Why do you compose?
What does the act of creating mean to you?

OLIVIER MESSIAEN. I have often been asked that question, and I
find it rather unprofitable; indeed, it seems to me that a
composer writes music because he must, because that is his
vocation and he does it very naturally, as an apple-tree bears
apples or a rose-bush roses.

It is certain that since childhood I've felt an irresistible and
overwhelming vocation for music. My parents were not at all
opposed to it: they themselves were artists. My father, Pierre
Messiaen, taught English, and left a critical translation of the
complete works of Shakespeare. My mother, Cécile Sauvage,
was a great poet of motherhood: she left (among other works) a
book of verse L'Ame en bourgeon ("The Soul in Travail") which
was dedicated to me before my birth and which influenced my
future.

I taught myself the piano during the war of 1914, when I was
in Grenoble. Then I began my first essays in composition, and
I've kept a piano piece from that time called La Dame de Shalott
after Tennyson's poem. It's obviously a very childish piece, but
neither quite silly nor completely devoid of sense. I still regard it
with a certain tenderness.

CLAUDE SAMUEL. Was the piece published?

OLIVIER MESSIAEN. Oh no! It's just the stammering of a child...

1

CLAUDE SAMUEL. If you've been composing ever since that time, it's obviously because an instinct has impelled you . . .

OLIVIER MESSIAEN. Certainly, and that's what I can't explain. That's why the question "Why do you write music?" seems pointless.

CLAUDE SAMUEL. It's undoubtedly pointless if one takes it in the sense of "Why did you begin to write music?", but let me make my question more precise: "Why do you write music *today*?"

OLIVIER MESSIAEN. When I was a child, music was a distraction, in the same way as toys are for other children, and, for me, a diversion—like the plays of Shakespeare which I declaimed complete before an audience of one (my brother) between the ages of five and eight. I stress this fact because it is bound up with music.

Today, I write as a professional, not only in my hours of relaxation as formerly. I'm obliged to fight fiercely for these creative periods, usually in the summer, and this task no longer has the same naïveté. I compose to defend something, to express something, to place something; and each new work obviously poses new problems, all the more complex in that our age has given birth to numerous contentious aesthetics. I try to become acquainted with them all and yet to remain quite outside them.

CLAUDE SAMUEL. What "expressions" then do you want to defend in writing music? What impressions do you want to communicate to your listeners?

OLIVIER MESSIAEN. The first idea that I wished to express—and the most important, because it stands above them all—is the existence of the truths of the Catholic faith. I've the good fortune to be a Catholic. I was born a believer, and it happens that the Scriptures struck me even as a child. So a number of my works are intended to bring out the theological truths of the Catholic faith. That is the first aspect of my work, the noblest and, doubtless, the most useful and valuable; perhaps the only one which I won't regret at the hour of my death. But I'm a human being and, like all human beings, I'm sensitive to human love. I've tried to express this in three of my works through the medium of the greatest myth of human love, that of Tristan and

Isolde. Finally, I have a profound love for nature. I think that nature infinitely surpasses us, and I've always sought lessons from it. By preference, I've loved birds, so I've examined birdsong especially: I've studied ornithology. There is in my music this juxtaposition of Catholic faith, the Tristan and Isolde myth and a highly developed use of birdsong.

CLAUDE SAMUEL. Let's speak first of the bonds that exist between your creative work and your Catholic faith. Would you have been able to compose if you hadn't felt this Catholic faith? Without it, would your music have been very different?

OLIVIER MESSIAEN. The question of aesthetic language and that of the sentiment expressed are two different spheres. I see the best proof of this in the fact that some well-known composers, Mozart for example, have been able to employ exactly the same musical language for works of very secular nature as well as for works of very religious character—succeeding in both cases without really altering their aesthetic canons.

CLAUDE SAMUEL. When you're writing a liturgical work yourself, do you use the same language as for a secular work?

OLIVIER MESSIAEN. Near enough. This, of course, scandalises some people. To me, it seems ridiculous and detrimental to contradict one's style and adopt different aesthetics under the pretext that the subject and idea to be expressed have changed.

CLAUDE SAMUEL. But there exist, it seems to me, two attitudes for a Catholic composer *vis-à-vis* his work: the first consists of writing music really intended for the liturgy, the second of creating works of religious character which are primarily concert works. Can't one distinguish these two tendencies in your output?

OLIVIER MESSIAEN. No. I've never written, for example, a traditional Mass, with Kyrie, Gloria, Sanctus and Agnus Dei, a liturgical piece perfectly appropriate to worship. I've only composed some long works for organ, lengthy cycles, suitable for performance during a Low Mass, which respect the main divisions of the Mass and comment on the texts relating to each of the Mysteries of Christ in the Proper of the Day and the prayers proceeding from it. On the other hand, I've imposed the

3

truths of the Faith on the concert room, but in a liturgical sense. Proof of this is that my main religious concert work is called *Trois petites Liturgies*. I didn't choose this title idly: I thought of performing a liturgical act, that is to say, transporting a kind of Office, a kind of organised act of praise into the concert room. This—I repeat—scandalised some people, but my chief originality is to have taken the idea of the Catholic liturgy from the stone buildings intended for religious services and to have installed it in other buildings not intended for this kind of music and which, finally, have received it very well.

CLAUDE SAMUEL. But let's take the very case of the *Petites Liturgies*. Do you prefer them to be given in a concert hall or in a church?

OLIVIER MESSIAEN. They are at home in both.

CLAUDE SAMUEL. So your religious works present an ambivalent character. But when you're an organist your musical activity is completely geared to the liturgy . . .

OLIVIER MESSIAEN. Of course! As I told you, my organ works can be played during a Low Mass and fit the different time divisions of the Office very closely.

CLAUDE SAMUEL. And doubtless you became an organist because of your Catholic faith?

OLIVIER MESSIAEN. Oh no! It's strange, but for years I just went to Mass as a parishioner, and I was sixteen or seventeen when my harmony professor, Jean Gallon, had the idea of introducing me to Marcel Dupré so that I might study the organ, not because I was a Catholic but because he sensed in me the gifts of an improviser. At the time, I had just won a prize in the piano accompaniment class. It was a class where one not only harmonised given melodies (which is an important part of improvisation at the piano) but also did sight-reading and score-reading. As I showed gifts in this field, and as the organ is essentially intended for improvisation, I was led to the organ class. Having won an organ prize, I thereupon quite naturally entered a church as a "liturgical official" and as a titular organist.

4

CLAUDE SAMUEL. And the first church was . . .

OLIVIER MESSIAEN. This first and only church is the Eglise de la Sainte-Trinité in Paris.

CLAUDE SAMUEL. How old were you when you went there?

OLIVIER MESSIAEN. I was very young: I was just twenty-two.

CLAUDE SAMUEL. You were the youngest titular organist in France, and since that date you have practically never ceased to be active as organist in this church . . .

OLIVIER MESSIAEN. I have been consistently and quite seriously active there for thirty-three years. Every Sunday I've played for three Masses and Vespers, and often funerals and weddings during the week. I stopped for a few years because, by order of the Paris civic authorities, the organ had to be repaired, but I took up my duties again as soon as the restoration was complete.

CLAUDE SAMUEL. On this organ at the Trinité, do you essentially play your written compositions or do you give yourself over to improvisation?

OLIVIER MESSIAEN. On account of the succession of different priests-in-charge at the Trinité, my services were rather wisely shared out: for the High Mass on Sunday, I played only plainsong, harmonised or not according to circumstances; for the eleven o'clock Mass on Sundays, classical and romantic music; for the Mass at noon, still on a Sunday, I was allowed to play my own music; and finally, for the five o'clock Vespers, I was obliged to improvise because the verses were too short to allow for the playing of pieces between the Psalms and during the Magnificat.

CLAUDE SAMUEL. What is your improvised music like? Is it nearer to your written music or to music more classical in character?

OLIVIER MESSIAEN. It was sometimes very classical in character, when circumstances constrained me; I developed the technique of making pastiches on purpose: mock-Mozart, mock-Bach, mock-Schumann and mock-Debussy, in order to continue in the same key and in the same style as the piece just sung. But, even so, I improvised in my own style, living on my harmonic and

5

rhythmic "fat"; sometimes I was lucky and had strokes of inspiration . . .

These inspirations went on for a long time, until the day I realised that they tired me out and that I was emptying all my substance into them. I then wrote the *Messe de la Pentecôte* which is a résumé of all my collected improvisations. The *Messe de la Pentecôte* was followed by the *Livre d'orgue*, which is a much more considered work, and after that, as it were, I've never improvised in my work.

CLAUDE SAMUEL. Weren't the various priests-in-charge you've known at the Trinité a bit startled by the introduction into their church of music as daring as that of the *Livre d'orgue?*

OLIVIER MESSIAEN. They weren't startled because the truths I express, the Truths of the Faith, *are* startling; they are fairy-tales, in turn mysterious, harrowing, glorious and sometimes terrifying, always based on a luminous, unchanging Reality. I am perforce a hundred thousand degrees below each Truth. No, the priests weren't startled, but the parishioners were, because they don't always know the texts they hear (although they hear them every Sunday), either because they don't understand Latin, or because they understand nothing at all, even if they're spoken to in French. But, I repeat, the various priests at the Trinité shared things out very wisely, adapting each style to the needs of each Office, and even to the needs of each congregation; for the public which comes to the Mass at noon is not that which attends the High Mass, and the public for Vespers is not that of the eleven o'clock Mass.

CLAUDE SAMUEL. I won't ask you to explain the secret reasons for your religious faith; instinct, you told us, plays the largest part in this. But isn't this faith also the echo of the attraction you feel for the marvellous, for mystery and for poetry?

OLIVIER MESSIAEN. Certainly! but in this I revert to the plays of Shakespeare which I recited as a child. You know all that is contained in Shakespeare's plays, not only human passions but also magicians, witches, sprites, phantoms and apparitions of all kinds. Shakespeare is an author who develops the imagination powerfully. I was inclined towards fairy-tales, and Shakespeare is sometimes a super-fairy-tale; it's this aspect of Shakespeare above all that impressed me, much more than certain disillusioned accents on love or death such as are found in *Hamlet*, accents which a child of eight obviously couldn't understand. I loved *Macbeth* best of all (because of the witches and Banquo's ghost), also Puck and Ariel (for similar reasons), and I felt very vividly the grandeur of the mad King Lear upbraiding the storm and lightning. As for the famous stage instruction in the historical plays, "alarums, skirmishes, the enemy enters the city", it has remained for me the symbol of the novelty to be achieved . . .

It's certain that in the truths of the Catholic faith I found this attraction of the marvellous multiplied a hundredfold, a thousandfold, and it's no longer a matter of theatrical fiction but of something real. *I chose what was true.* In the manner of St Christopher who, when he was called Reprobus, served in succession the Queen of Voluptuousness, the King of Gold and finally carried Christ (whence his name of Christophorus: 'Christ-bearer').

CLAUDE SAMUEL. It's very strange to realise the importance of the theatre in your life and particularly during your childhood, whereas in your composing career you've never written for the theatre; on the other hand, in your works you've widely used these marvels which you've found in the Catholic faith.

OLIVIER MESSIAEN. I have sought to express the marvels of the Faith. I won't say that I've succeeded, for in the last analysis they're inexpressible. In other respects, I've always loved the theatre, and still do today, but my first love is the spoken play. Of course, I give my pupils courses on all kinds of opera and operatic aesthetics, from Monteverdi to *Pelléas* and *Wozzeck*, by way of Rameau, Mozart, Wagner and Mussorgsky, but these aesthetics have now been overtaken. They gave rise to total successes which cannot be re-worked, and it seems to me that music drama is always a kind of betrayal.

I would add that most of the arts are unsuited to the expression of religious truths: only music, the most immaterial of all, comes closest to it. But on the stage of a theatre, one is

7

placed so far below the chosen subject that one runs the risk of foundering in the ridiculous, the unseemly, or the absurd.

CLAUDE SAMUEL. It must be recognised that religious music is often rather feeble, whereas your approach consists in rediscovering the violence contained in the Holy Scriptures.

OLIVIER MESSIAEN. I haven't rediscovered it. It exists and I've expressed it such as it is. This rather feeble music you speak of is the result of conventions and errors which, unfortunately, are all too widespread.

CLAUDE SAMUEL. And what's to be said of some liturgical music that is more liturgical than musical?

OLIVIER MESSIAEN. Truly liturgical music, that which is intended to accompany the Office, is, for all that, an extremely well-founded act of praise in its origin, and those who accomplish this act of praise do so with excellent intention.

CLAUDE SAMUEL. In your opinion, who are the classical composers who have best served religious faith?

OLIVIER MESSIAEN. It's very difficult to answer . . . There's probably only one really religious music, because it's detached from all exterior effect and all intention, and that's plainsong.

CLAUDE SAMUEL. We'd like you to give us a lesson on plainsong, but that would be straying too far from our subject. Let's return, if we may, to those three main lines of force which inform all your output: Catholic faith, the "Tristans" and Nature. You have recalled your attitude as a Catholic in regard to music: let's speak now of the "Tristans".

OLIVIER MESSIAEN. I've composed three "Tristans", very different in dimension and instrumental media: the earliest is *Harawi*, an hour-long song cycle with piano; the second is the *Turangalîla Symphony*, for Ondes Martenot, piano solo and very large orchestra, lasting about an hour and a quarter; and finally the *Cinq Rechants* for a choir of twelve unaccompanied voices which should last from twenty to twenty-five minutes.

CLAUDE SAMUEL. The nature of these works implies a direct reference to the Tristan legend. How do you imagine this legend?

OLIVIER MESSIAEN. One might say that this legend is the symbol

8

of all great loves and of all great love poems in literature or music. But only the Tristan myth seemed worthy of attention; in no way did I want to re-work Wagner's *Tristan und Isolde* or Debussy's *Pelléas*, to mention only the two greatest "Tristans" in music.

CLAUDE SAMUEL. Your "Tristans" don't place characters on a stage...

OLIVIER MESSIAEN. No, mine have absolutely no connection with the old Celtic legend, and even its essential idea of a love-potion is brushed aside (except for some allusions in the *Cinq Rechants*). I've kept only the idea of a love that is fatal, irresistible and which, as a rule, leads to death; a love which, to some extent, invokes death, for it transcends the body—even the limits of the mind—and extends on a cosmic scale.

CLAUDE SAMUEL. Isn't this idea of human love in contradiction to your religious faith?

OLIVIER MESSIAEN. No, because a great love is a reflection—a pale reflection, but nevertheless a reflection—of the only true love, Divine Love.

CLAUDE SAMUEL. Do you think that in one and the same work the Tristan idea can be associated with religious faith?

OLIVIER MESSIAEN. Can one place a human symbol beside an Eternal Truth? That would be scandalous arrogance! But right away you must discard the notion—yours, perhaps, which is false—of the eternal theatrical triangle of Mr, Mrs, and the lover; I never dreamt of that in thinking about Tristan, and the idea of prohibition or punishment has no place there.

CLAUDE SAMUEL. Yet Tristan is nevertheless just that...

OLIVIER MESSIAEN. Yes, because it's the contradiction which gives birth to great love and which leads to death; but the essential idea is not the contradiction, but the great love and the death which follows. There is in this an initiation, by death and separation from the world, into a greater and purer love which perhaps the mention of other myths will help you understand better: I think of the airy prison in which Viviane confines Merlin, or the descent of Orpheus into Hades...

9

CLAUDE SAMUEL.   So your Tristan symbolises the purity of love. Doesn't this conception of human love superimposed upon your Catholic faith explain the third aspect of your musical personality: the man of nature? It seems to me that a hidden but real bond unites these three constituents of your artistic expression.

OLIVIER MESSIAEN. The phenomenon of nature is indeed marvellously beautiful and calming, and, for me, ornithological work is not only an element of consolation in my researches into musical aesthetics, but also a factor of health. It's perhaps thanks to this work that I've been able to resist the misfortunes and complications of life.

CLAUDE SAMUEL.   At what period were you attracted by nature?

OLIVIER MESSIAEN.   As with music and faith: always. But my strongest feelings about nature, those I remember most vividly, date back to my adolescence, to the age of fourteen or fifteen. Previously, there were perhaps others: they remain confused for they date back to a time when I was very young. When I was three or four we lived in Ambert, where my father had his first appointment as a teacher of English, and there I obviously experienced the revelation of nature, but this revelation remained unconscious and I haven't retained any precise memories of it. So my memories go back to the age of fourteen or fifteen, chiefly to a period when I went and stayed in the Aube with aunts who owned a somewhat odd farm, with sculptures by one of my uncles, a flower-bed, an orchard, some cows and hens. All this was very varied, and, to "restore" my health, my good aunts would send me to tend a little herd of cows; it was really a tiny little herd (there were only three cows) but even so I tended them very badly. One day they managed to escape and wrought terrible havoc in a field of beetroot, which they devoured in a few hours, earning me the reproaches of all the villagers.

The Aube countryside is very beautiful and very simple with its plain, big fields surrounded by trees, magnificent dawns and sunsets, and a great number of birds. It was there that I first began noting down birdsong. I was obviously a beginner and I noted things of which I understood nothing, not even being able to identify the bird that was singing.

CLAUDE SAMUEL. We'll speak later of ornithology, but I want to ask you if, despite yourself, you're not in the last resort a townsman.

OLIVIER MESSIAEN. Yes, despite myself. I have an absolute horror of cities, a horror of the one I live in, despite its many beauties—I speak of the French capital—and a horror of all the bad taste man has accumulated around him, whether for his needs or for various other reasons. You'll notice, as I do, that there are never any errors of taste in nature; you'll never find a fault in lighting or colouring or, in birdsong, an error in rhythm, melody or counterpoint.

CLAUDE SAMUEL. It seems to me that we link up here with your Catholic faith. You think that the divine mystery of creation is responsible for the perfect harmony in nature?

OLIVIER MESSIAEN. Absolutely. Nature has kept a purity, a springing forth, a freshness which we have lost.

CLAUDE SAMUEL. So this word "purity", which you invoke, as much in your Catholic faith as in the "Tristans", reappears in your love for nature: this quest for purity, isn't it the outstanding feature of your human and musical personality?

OLIVIER MESSIAEN. That's possible. I wouldn't have thought of saying it, but you say it and it must be true.

CLAUDE SAMUEL. Is your love of nature closely linked to your Catholic faith?

OLIVIER MESSIAEN. Linked, yet at the same time independent. I love nature for itself. Certainly, like St Paul, I see in nature a manifestation of one of the aspects of divinity, but it's equally certain that God's creations are not God himself. Moreover, all God's creations are enclosed in Time, and Time is one of God's strangest creatures because it is totally opposed to Him who is Eternal by nature, to Him who is without beginning, end, or succession.

CLAUDE SAMUEL. Which aspect of nature do you prefer? Mountain, sea or countryside?

OLIVIER MESSIAEN. I love all nature, and I love all landscapes,

11

but I have a predilection for mountains, because I passed my childhood at Grenoble, and saw, from my earliest years, the mountains of the Dauphiné . . .

CLAUDE SAMUEL. Like Berlioz . . .

OLIVIER MESSIAEN. Like Berlioz—and the especially wild places which are the most beautiful in France, like the Glacier de la Meije—less famous than Mont Blanc but certainly more terrible, purer, more apart . . .

CLAUDE SAMUEL. You love nature in its wildest manifestations . . .

OLIVIER MESSIAEN. In its most secret and grandiose aspects, and, let me admit, when unsullied by man.

CLAUDE SAMUEL. And have you been struck during your travels by landscapes completely different from those you knew in your childhood and in your youth?

OLIVIER MESSIAEN. Certainly. During journeys which were the starting point of certain pieces in my *Catalogue d'Oiseaux*, "Le Merle Bleu", "Le Traquet rieur", and "Le Traquet stapazin", I got to know the region of the Pyrénées Orientales, and it was love at first sight; from the first instant I was enraptured by this extraordinary region which combines the blue of the sea, overhanging cliffs, terraced vineyards, forests of cork-oak and even everlasting snows.

CLAUDE SAMUEL. Do you regard nature as an object, a living manifestation, or as a vehicle for feelings? Do you subscribe to the opinion of the romantics which perceives a consoling strength in nature?

OLIVIER MESSIAEN. I see nothing of all that. Nature is primarily a very great power in which one can lose oneself, a kind of nirvana, but above all it's a marvellous teacher, and this last aspect of it has been very useful to my work.

CLAUDE SAMUEL. For you, then, nature's first contribution is to provide sounds?

OLIVIER MESSIAEN. Absolutely.

CLAUDE SAMUEL. Not limited only to birdsong . . .

OLIVIER MESSIAEN. Not limited only to birdsong! I've listened with intense emotion to the waves of the sea, to mountain torrents and waterfalls, and to all the sounds made by water and wind. And I would add that I make no distinction between noise and sound: for me, all this always represents music.

CLAUDE SAMUEL. In composing, do you try to reproduce the sounds of nature?

OLIVIER MESSIAEN. I've tried, and I've addressed myself to birdsong, because that, finally, is the most musical, the nearest to us, and the easiest to reproduce. The sounds of wind and water are extraordinarily complex. On the other hand, they have long been listened to and captured by composers such as Berlioz, Wagner and, above all, Debussy, who was the great lover of wind and water. But I'm bound to say that none of them was completely successful in penetrating the details of these complex sounds and complexes of sound. And, personally, I feel totally incapable of it: it's terribly difficult.

CLAUDE SAMUEL. But the modern composer is perhaps better equipped for this task . . .

OLIVIER MESSIAEN. Yes, because if need be he can use a tape-recorder and with the help of electronic apparatus he can dissect what he has recorded.

CLAUDE SAMUEL. Have you tried this experiment?

OLIVIER MESSIAEN. No, I've never used a tape-recorder, even for birdsong. I write quite simply with pencil and manuscript paper, as if I were taking down a *solfège* dictation.

CLAUDE SAMUEL. What do you think of Debussy's phrase: "To see daybreak is more useful than listening to the Pastoral Symphony"?

OLIVIER MESSIAEN. It's a sally of no great consequence. But it does show that he placed nature above all. Besides, Debussy was a composer who understood the sound-colour relationship which I myself feel so intensely, and he understood it by contemplating nature.

CLAUDE SAMUEL. For you, a composer, is the presence of colour in nature then as essential as that of sound?

OLIVIER MESSIAEN. Both are linked. Without suffering from synopsia (as did my friend the painter Blanc-Gatti, who had a disorder of the optic and aural nerves which allowed him really

13

to see colours and shapes when he heard music), when I hear a score or read it, hearing it in my mind, I also see in my mind's eye corresponding colours which turn, mix and blend with each other just like the sounds which turn, mix and intermingle, and at the same time as them . . .

CLAUDE SAMUEL. Is it nature that has given you your love of colours?

OLIVIER MESSIAEN. Nature, and also stained glass when I was a child. At the time when my father was appointed a teacher in Paris, I took great delight in visiting monuments, museums and churches: my first visits to Notre-Dame, the Sainte-Chapelle, and later to the cathedrals of Chartres and Bourges, certainly exercised an influence on my career. I've remained dazzled for ever by the marvellous colours of this mediaeval stained glass.

CLAUDE SAMUEL. In fact, cathedral stained glass represents a human creation which you don't deny, you who detest towns and artificial creations. Stained glass, then, is a creation noble enough to equal that of nature?

OLIVIER MESSIAEN. But it's nature's own most extraordinary manifestation: it's *light* caught by man to glorify the most noble of functional sites, the buildings intended for worship.

CLAUDE SAMUEL. In speaking of nature, we revert then to your Catholic faith, just as a moment ago when recalling the "Tristans" we also spoke of nature and Catholic faith. All this clearly indicates that your personality is crystallised around these three ideas which perhaps appear essentially opposed but are in fact very close.

OLIVIER MESSIAEN. And they are resolved finally in one and the same idea: Divine Love!

Conversation 2

CLAUDE SAMUEL. Your book *Technique de mon langage musical* ("Technique of My Musical Language") represents the sum of your musical language. What is the book's significance now?

OLIVIER MESSIAEN. It's now out of date; much of its content is still valid, but it's nearly thirty years since I wrote it. At that time, everything concerning rhythm was very new. So were the modes of limited transposition which were, in the realm of sound, the equivalent of non-retrogradable rhythms in the realm of time. Today, I no longer use these things. I am actually preparing a new work, much more complete than the first, which will be devoted entirely to rhythm and entitled *Traité de rythme* ("Treatise on Rhythm").

CLAUDE SAMUEL. We will raise the problems of rhythm later, but, for the moment, to grasp your musical personality more completely, I'd like you to revert to this question which is so curious and yet so important in your aesthetic: the rôle you attribute in your music to colour.

OLIVIER MESSIAEN. For the composer, there are different ways of conceiving colour. The first and most interesting is that which we have mentioned earlier, that is to say the sound-colour relationship perceived psychologically. I spoke to you of my friend, the Swiss painter Blanc-Gatti, who suffered from synopsia. I have at home two or three of his pictures, unfortunately only in reproduction: he has fixed on to the canvas a very brief and fugitive moment, some colours so glimpsed, for of course these colours turn and mix and intermingle exactly like sounds. These pictures are, however,

15

very revealing of a certain aspect of colour linked to sound. I might add that Blanc-Gatti's disease can be contracted in a rather simple if expensive manner, by going to Mexico and swallowing a noxious drink called mescalin, which comes from a small cactus, the Peyote (or *Echinocactus Williamsi*), which was a sacred plant in Ancient Mexico and still grows there. The Mexican priests and initiates used it for religious or prophetic ends connected with the solar myth. Absorbing the alkaloid produced by this plant induces a loss of the sense of time, minutes seeming like centuries, and above all it produces coloured visions.

CLAUDE SAMUEL. Visions which deform colours?

OLIVIER MESSIAEN. Not at all. Visions superimposed on to natural surroundings. Anyone placed under the influence of the drug loses neither sight nor reason. He always sees what is around him, but coloured visions are superimposed on to whatever surrounds him; he also experiences visions linked to the hearing of sounds, even if these aren't musical. Thus the simple creaking of a door or the rubbing of two branches in the forest can engender in the patient these coloured visions which apparently seem ineffable, marvellous, grandiose and in perpetual motion, moving with extreme, even feverish rapidity. These are colours which turn and return many times before the patient's eye.

CLAUDE SAMUEL. You say "apparently": you don't know this from personal experience?

OLIVIER MESSIAEN. Obviously: I've never taken mescalin!

CLAUDE SAMUEL. Haven't you been tempted?

OLIVIER MESSIAEN. No, because it's dangerous. It's a narcotic for which one could acquire a taste. But it's extraordinary that, having neither absorbed this drug nor yet having the disease of my painter friend, I am all the same affected by a kind of synopsia, found more in my mind than in my body, which allows me, when I hear music, and equally when I read it, to see inwardly, in the mind's eye, colours which move with the music, and I sense these colours in an extremely vivid manner. and I've sometimes even precisely indicated these corres-

16

pondences in my scores. One should of course be able to prove this relationship scientifically, but I'm incapable of it.

CLAUDE SAMUEL. Do you *see* these colours, or do you imagine them?

OLIVIER MESSIAEN. I see them inwardly: this is not imagination, nor is it a psychic phenomenon. It's an inward reality.

CLAUDE SAMUEL. So, when a door creaks, you see a colour?

OLIVIER MESSIAEN. No, this correspondence is related to real music with melodies, chords, rhythms, and complexes of sounds and durations.

CLAUDE SAMUEL. And you've always been subject to this rather exceptional phenomenon?

OLIVIER MESSIAEN. I think so.

CLAUDE SAMUEL. But do you try to translate colours in your music?

OLIVIER MESSIAEN. Actually I try to translate colours into music: for me certain complexes of sound and certain sonorities are linked to complexes of colour, and I use them in full knowledge of this.

CLAUDE SAMUEL. Have you yet composed a work in which you draw your inspiration from the contemplation of the colours of a painting?

OLIVIER MESSIAEN. No, never, I repeat that for me certain sonorities are linked with certain complexes of colour and I use them as colours, juxtaposing them and putting them in relief against each other, as a painter underlines one colour with its complementary.

CLAUDE SAMUEL. Haven't you ever wanted to paint?

OLIVIER MESSIAEN. In my childhood, when 1 was reading Shakespeare, I made some theatre sets in a way that linked with my love for stained glass: as a backcloth I used cellophane which I found in sweet-boxes or in cake containers and I would brush it with Chinese ink or just water-colours; then I placed my décors in front of a window-pane and the sun passing through the coloured cellophane would produce luminous and coloured projections on the floor of my little theatre as well as

17

on the *dramatis personae*. Thus I managed to transform my décors just as an electrician controls lighting in a theatre.

CLAUDE SAMUEL. Other composers have tried to establish relationships between colour, or luminous colour, and music: I'm thinking of Scriabin or even more of Schoenberg who, in *Die glückliche Hand*, prescribed exactly the coloured projections which should accompany the staging of that opera. Can this be ascribed to the same approach?

OLIVIER MESSIAEN. Certainly, and you'll notice in regard to the musical stage that for a long time composers worried little about the lighting which would accompany the unfolding of their music. It's with Mozart that we begin to perceive a premeditated connection. The churchyard scene with the Commendatore in *Don Giovanni* instigates a completely new and absolutely inspired departure from the usual for the period, not only because the character is awe-inspiring and the subject terrifying, but because at that moment the reign of night over the scene is underlined by supernatural lighting: all this is conveyed by the orchestration and also by the chord-colouring. In this scene there are inversions of the chords of the diminished seventh and diminished fifth with an altered third which would be taken up by Chopin as "colour" and be used by Debussy under the title of "whole-tone scale". Later, Wagner freely employed certain chords and black sonorities in scenes taking place at night, for dark characters like the Nibelung Alberich and his son Hagen; and in contradistinction, bright tonalities and chords with lightened, sharper instrumentation for events taking place on mountain heights or in water, like Siegfried discovering the happy mountains before encountering love in Brünnhilde, or the Rhinemaidens swimming in the Rhine.

CLAUDE SAMUEL. Then this idea of colour is implicitly linked with music in the work of many great classical composers.

OLIVIER MESSIAEN. Yes, and those who didn't realise it committed a grave error. It may be of course that the composer didn't foresee the result. But I'll give you a little instance to prove to you to what extent I've always been sensitive to the sound-colour relationship, and this almost unconsciously at the beginning. Once I attended the ballet in a small town the name of which I've forgotten. It was a ballet to music by Beethoven; a quite haphazard arrangement, and, rather arbitrarily, the scenario comprised a kind of romantic legend in the style of Musset with a charming décor showing a garden in moonlight with violet lighting and a fountain. Now, the Beethoven music was in G major . . . I don't know whether you realise that the colour violet and G major produce an absolutely terrifying dissonance! I'm not speaking of the error in setting a romantic legend complete with fountain to music by Beethoven (which is stupid) but of the juxtaposition of the colour violet and chords of G major: this clashed in a terrible manner and gave me stomach ache.

CLAUDE SAMUEL. What's the key that marries best with violet?

OLIVIER MESSIAEN. One really can't talk of an exact correspondence between a key and a colour: that would be a rather naïve way of expressing oneself because, I repeat, colours are complex and are linked to equally complex chords and sounds. In my early works, I often used what I called "modes of limited transposition". The two main modes are linked for me to very precise colourings: Mode No. 2 revolves around certain violets, blues and violet-purple, whilst Mode No. 3 corresponds to an orange with red and green pigments, patches of gold and also a milky white with iridescent opal-like reflections.

CLAUDE SAMUEL. Does this correspondence between sound and colour rest on scientific fact, or is it the result of a totally subjective estimation?

OLIVIER MESSIAEN. I think it rests on scientific fact modified by the personality of whoever is subject to the phenomenon, to which may be added something of imagination and of literary influence difficult to express.

CLAUDE SAMUEL. What are your favourites in the immense range of colours?

OLIVIER MESSIAEN. Ever since my birth I've been devoted to violet; it seems that this is a normal phenomenon, for I was born under the sign of Sagittarius.

CLAUDE SAMUEL. Are there colours to which you're allergic?

19

OLIVIER MESSIAEN. Yes, I don't like yellow very much.

CLAUDE SAMUEL. You allude to a pure colour, but I know that you prefer subtle and very complex colours.

OLIVIER MESSIAEN. I spoke to you of violet; now, violet is a complex colour because it blends blue, an extremely cold colour, with red, an extremely warm colour; but violet is capable of many nuances: there is, for example, a violet in which red dominates and which is called purple, and, at the other end of the scale, there's a violet containing more blue than red, called hyacinth-blue. These two violets have a great importance: in the Middle Ages, in symbolism and in stained glass, the one represented the Love of Truth and the other the Truth of Love. And this reversal of terms is certainly not just a play on words but corresponds without doubt very closely to these nuances of violet.

CLAUDE SAMUEL. Don't you think that this correspondence of feelings or ideas with colours is based on a superstition?

OLIVIER MESSIAEN. What superstition?

CLAUDE SAMUEL. A popular belief in the benevolent or malevolent power of certain colours . . .

OLIVIER MESSIAEN. The mediaeval masters of stained glass passed on secrets from father to son, for the same reason as the master architects and master masons. There could be some influence of magic here or of primitive initiations, but this doesn't gainsay that the symbolism is of great beauty and has produced extraordinary results. One must bow before the stained glass of Bourges, the rose-windows of Notre-Dame or the great windows of Chartres.

CLAUDE SAMUEL. To understand your love of colours better, independently of psychic and psychological phenomena, should one recall the allure magic has for you?

OLIVIER MESSIAEN. You're plumbing dangerous depths in me there! As a Catholic I should have no right to speak of magic; but let's admit, it's not devoid of interest. I'm not speaking of black magic and of people who cast spells—that's just a joke—but there does exist a white magic, and that's a symbolical quest for the power of language, sounds or colours, for the influence of certain things we own or which surround us.

CLAUDE SAMUEL. After that brief trip into the world of magic, let's return, if we may, to your love of colours. How do you place yourself in relation to painters?

OLIVIER MESSIAEN. I prefer one painter to all others, not only because he was the precursor of abstract painting, and consequently very close to what I see when I hear music, but above all because he established in a very subtle and forceful manner the rapports between complementary colours, especially by the principle of "simultaneous contrast" and *Orphisme:* that painter is Robert Delaunay.

CLAUDE SAMUEL. Is it possible to establish rapports on the aesthetic plane between composers and painters?

OLIVIER MESSIAEN. The rapport between sound and colour does exist, but composers and painters belong to two very different categories, and the fact that the one serves sound and the other colour does not imply that they shall be brothers.

CLAUDE SAMUEL. Then let's forget the chances of this fraternisation. I would nevertheless point out to you that it's odd for a composer to explain the sources of his language by speaking first of all about colour. Leaving colour aside, let's now consider the specifically musical basis of your art and, in the first place, the structure of your harmonic vocabulary.

OLIVIER MESSIAEN. Then let's begin at the beginning! First of all, I must speak to you about a phenomenon which, if I may say so, has dominated all my composing life, and which I perhaps rather naïvely called in my first treatise "the charm of impossibilities". I've always thought that a technical process would possess much more power—and (reverting to magic) a quasi-occult power—the more it came up, in its very essence, against an insuperable obstacle. This is exactly the case in my three principal innovations: firstly, in the harmonic field, the "modes of limited transposition", transposable in a limited number of cases because they already contain tiny transpositions within themselves.—Secondly . . .

21

CLAUDE SAMUEL. I must interrupt you. Could you explain this technical detail to music-lovers without any precise musical knowledge?

OLIVIER MESSIAEN. That is perhaps possible by just explaining to them that our tempered music comprises twelve semitones, and that the number twelve is obtained by the following multiplications: three times four, four times three, twice six, and six times two. The modes of limited transposition are divided into symmetrical groups, the last note of each group being the same as the first of the following group. These groups are organised in six groups of two notes, four groups of three notes, three groups of four notes, and two groups in which the number of notes is variable. It follows that, after a certain number of transpositions, these modes arrive back at the same series of notes, and, consequently, it's impossible to transpose any further.

The "modes of limited transposition" correspond to another innovation in the field of rhythm, that of "non-retrogradable" rhythms. The modes of limited transposition can't be transposed because they contain tiny transpositions within themselves, and non-retrogradable rhythms can't be reversed because they contain a tiny retrogression within themselves.

Finally, I've used in all my latest works, notably *Chronochromie*, another innovation which I call "symmetrical permutations". This is the same phenomenon: the unfolding of permutations in a certain order of reading, which is always the same, results in a limited number of permutations and, instead of reaching absolutely astronomical figures, one is stopped because one arrives once again at the chromatic sequence of note-values and the first permutation.

That is "the charm of impossibilities". They possess an occult power, a calculated ascendancy in time and sound. It's said that some of my works have a spell-binding power over the public. There's nothing of the magician about me, and this spell-binding power doesn't come stupidly from repetitions, as has been pretended, but perhaps from these impossibilities enclosed within this or that formula.

CLAUDE SAMUEL. Have you consciously used these modes of limited transposition from the beginning?

OLIVIER MESSIAEN. It was an unconscious step at first; later, I became aware of their power and ability, and I tried to explain this power to myself and to others. Some have spoken, with just cause, of the harmonic use of these modes: indeed, some people think of the modes as ladders, scales going up and down—especially down—whereas I do not use my modes melodically. I would go as far as to say that I use them as colours. They are not harmonies in the classical sense of the term. They are not even recognised chords. They are colours and their power springs primarily from the impossibility of transpositions and also to the colour linked with this impossibility. The two phenomena are simultaneous.

CLAUDE SAMUEL. How do you place yourself in regard to classical tonality?

OLIVIER MESSIAEN. There are tonal passages in my works but they are precisely blended with these modes which colour them and finally they have little importance. Some of my later works also include note-rows, but they haven't anything like the sound one would expect to find in a serial development, nor have they the "serial spirit"; they remain coloured because, fired by my love for colour, I treat them as colours.

CLAUDE SAMUEL. But, harmonically speaking, you are more of a modal composer?

OLIVIER MESSIAEN. Yes. I've happened to use the twelve notes in bundles and they sound quite unlike a series or a truncated series: they sound like colours. Sometimes I've used successions of chords where the twelve notes are heard simultaneously a great number of times, and nobody has noticed this. Perfect chords are heard and it is their arrangement which, placing one note or another in the limelight, changes its colour.

CLAUDE SAMUEL. Do you think that a composer can still use today the tonal language which has been in use for nearly three centuries?

OLIVIER MESSIAEN. I'm going to make you jump. I consider that the terms "tonal", "modal", "serial" and other words of this kind are illusory and that their use is based on a misconception; they are phenomena which have probably never existed; they've been exploited in books because lovely theories can be drawn up with pretty synoptic tables. But these are unimportant things, as composers have finally found out. Do you think that if the only quality of Mozart's Symphony in G minor was being in G minor anything would remain of it? . . .

CLAUDE SAMUEL.   Yes, but it is based on a tonal language . . .

OLIVIER MESSIAEN.   It is written in G minor, but the important point is its thematic and harmonic material, its rhythms and its accents. That it's in G minor matters little!

CLAUDE SAMUEL.   I'll be very cautious then! And yet, I seem to discern a natural evolution in that composers have long used a tonal language which has arrived at a period of decadence and today only a few composers use it. Does this analysis strike you as false?

OLIVIER MESSIAEN.   It's not entirely false. Let's say that it's an historical phenomenon spoken of complacently, for it's a handy way of presenting things; but one should go back further and say that all the music of antiquity was based on a modal language. Antiquity goes a very long way back . . . whereas classical tonal language has only lasted three centuries at most, and the so-called actual serial language—how long has that been with us? Thirty years . . . and even this is an exaggeration. And what distortions have been made of one system or the other! Let's take the example of Mozart again: he's said to be tonal! Marvellous passages like the Andante of the Concerto in E flat, K.482, the scene with the Commendatore in *Don Giovanni*, the scene with the rout of all the nocturnal characters (the Queen of the Night and her henchmen) in *The Magic Flute*, are not tonal, they're chromatic. Monteverdi, who is placed at the beginning of tonality, is he tonal? Never! He's chromatic. And Wagner, who's said to have corrupted tonality, he too is chromatic.

CLAUDE SAMUEL.   But chromaticism is a way of using tonality.

OLIVIER MESSIAEN.   Yes, but the series is also chromaticism and a mode is a choice within chromaticism.

24

CLAUDE SAMUEL. Aren't you making everything a question of terminology?

OLIVIER MESSIAEN. Certainly, because I find that these terms make an improper, though perhaps useful, means of dividing phenomena which are basically linked.

CLAUDE SAMUEL. After this interesting diversion, let's return to your language. We spoke of the relationship between colours and your harmonic vocabulary, but there's another transposition of colour and sound in your creative work. I'm thinking of your orchestration.

OLIVIER MESSIAEN. It's true that we haven't yet spoken about the colours of timbres which are so important. My way of orchestrating is, indeed, rather special. I use timbres in groups or in opposition like the classics, incorporating into them melodies of timbres as advocated by Schoenberg and realised by Webern and, above all, by more recent composers like Boulez, Stockhausen and the young Jean-Claude Eloy. But by availing myself of a timbre or group of timbres, I transform their colour by the sounds used and by the complexes of sounds used. A perfect chord written for a group of wind instruments doesn't sound like a more complex chord, and the timbre of the wind instruments can be completely transformed by this more complex chord, for it mustn't be forgotten that timbre is the result of a choice of the harmonics; if you add or subtract this harmonic or the other, it is obvious that the timbres themselves will be very much altered.

CLAUDE SAMUEL. When you're composing a work, you think immediately of the timbres that you will choose? I mean to say, you're not content to write a work at the piano and to orchestrate it the second time round?

OLIVIER MESSIAEN. That way of writing music twice, by dividing the task, was perhaps possible at the time of Rossini, but it's absolutely unthinkable today when orchestration is closely bound to composition.

CLAUDE SAMUEL. Isn't one of the principal innovations of present-day music, then, the acquisition of different timbres which will enrich orchestration?

25

OLIVIER MESSIAEN. Yes; we began to be aware of the territory of timbre with Berlioz, the father of modern orchestration. Berlioz was the first to understand the role of timbre and of specific timbre; for, previously—and I think of composers of genius like Bach and Handel and their contemporaries—timbres were interchangeable and one didn't hesitate to entrust a violin solo to an oboe, to transcribe an organ chorale for choir, to let a soprano sing a melody initially given to a flute, and so forth. There was in this sense a certain contempt for timbre.

CLAUDE SAMUEL. Wasn't the reason simply mundane? Composers wrote for the instruments at their disposal and thought of eventual modifications to the orchestral complement . . .

OLIVIER MESSIAEN. I don't think so. There is, all the same, in the history of music an ordered succession of events. In Western civilisation, in any case, melody appeared first, then harmony, and later the care for rhythm for which I am a little responsible, and finally there's a characteristic known for long in the Orient but which is quite recent in the West: the care for nuance and tempo, the oppositions and combinations of nuance and tempo.

CLAUDE SAMUEL. You think, then, that through its evolution music has enriched itself . . .

OLIVIER MESSIAEN. Certainly!

CLAUDE SAMUEL. Don't you think that it gains in one respect what it loses in another?

OLIVIER MESSIAEN. Perhaps it loses in simplicity, but it gains in a diversity of riches.

CLAUDE SAMUEL. But the polyphonies of the fourteenth century were very rich and very complex.

OLIVIER MESSIAEN. At the time of Machaut and particularly with his successors, there were indeed some very extraordinary researches into combining rhythms; proportional notation, when it first appeared, filled composers with joy, and they floundered mathematically in the novelty; then this frenzy calmed down and music was purified to become the harmonic music we know from the classical era. In the twentieth century we have rejoined the successors of Machaut and some are behaving a little in the same manner; they flounder joyfully in gimmicks which they don't really understand.

CLAUDE SAMUEL. Which shows an immoderate love for complexity. But to return to orchestration, there exists today a very special search for the aptness of timbre to the ensemble of musical phenomena.

OLIVIER MESSIAEN. This aptness of timbre and its specificity are extremely important ideas which, I repeat, date from Berlioz. He was the first to realise that a cor anglais solo was a solo for cor anglais and not for any other instrument.

CLAUDE SAMUEL. Can you give us some examples in the work of Berlioz?

OLIVIER MESSIAEN. But his work is full of absolutely perfect examples. I'll cite you a particularly fine one: the entry of the bell at the end of the *Symphonie Fantastique*. No other instrument could achieve the effect of terror and solitude better than a bell. The use of silence by Beethoven is equally extraordinary. In a sense, this also is part of the orchestration . . .

CLAUDE SAMUEL. And of the rhythm. . . .

OLIVIER MESSIAEN. In any case, before Berlioz there was little exploration in this field. Debussy took it up and Boulez thinks a great deal about timbre. Finally, beyond specific timbres used in orchestration, there's also the way of treating groups, of opposing them, disposing of them, taking account of those instruments that are weak and those that are strong, the solo registers and the secondary registers of each instrument, the possibility of effects disguising one instrument as another. The classical composers were not at all concerned with these ideas which Berlioz discovered.

CLAUDE SAMUEL. In the matter of orchestration, one's deep-seated nature also plays an essential role. Some composers are not sensitive to the beauties of orchestration whereas there's a whole family of composers who can be called "composer-orchestrators"; now, it's obvious that Berlioz belongs to this family, and so, on several counts, composers like Richard Strauss, Stravinsky and yourself can claim a place there.

OLIVIER MESSIAEN. Without doubt . . . But take care of the term "orchestrator"! Some composers whom I won't name trade as orchestrators, but their orchestra has no colour and doesn't "sound"; I hope that mine is colourful.

CLAUDE SAMUEL. I mean to say that some composers' orchestrations bear their signature: Berlioz and Strauss can be recognised from their manner of orchestrating, and you yourself may be recognised as much in the way you orchestrate as in an harmonic arrangement or rhythmic formula.

OLIVIER MESSIAEN. I hope so.

CLAUDE SAMUEL. Orchestration then is at the very centre of your creative act, and, if your different works are considered, a breakdown in the make-up of the classical orchestra is apparent. How do you explain this phenomenon?

OLIVIER MESSIAEN. There are several causes. One of the very first, and this may appear strange, is my love for the piano. The piano which *a priori* seems an instrument without timbres, is precisely, because of its lack of personality, an instrument favourable to a quest for timbres, for timbre doesn't come from the instrument but from the player. So it is as mobile as the playing. And it's because I love the piano and have played it a lot that I've been led to create not melodies of timbre but melodies of complexes of timbres.

The second cause is perhaps the fact that apart from my love for the piano—my favourite instrument—I was by profession an organist. You know there are three families of timbres in an organ: the foundation stops, the reeds, and the mixtures. The foundation stops are, properly speaking, the true organ timbre—flute sounds, if you wish; the reeds are trumpet timbres—the timbre of brass; but the third family is peculiar to the organ and exists nowhere else. These are the mixtures, single mutation stops or compound. You know that essentially mixtures are stops sounding other notes than those played. So that when you play middle C with a *cornet* stop, you hear, at the same time as that C, its octave, its twelfth, its fifteenth and its seventeenth—what is called a "four-foot" stop for the octave, "nazard" stop for the twelfth, "doublette" for the fifteenth, and "tierce" for the seventeenth. Now, these are harmonics man has produced by means of pipes added to a pipe sounding the fundamental.

In the classics of organ music these ensembles of harmonics were always used with the fundamental sound. But you'll admit that all the same it's a great temptation for a modern composer smitten with changes to eliminate the fundamental note: that's what I've done. I've used the organ mixtures with their false fifths, their false thirds, their false octaves, but without the fundamental notes, which has created a fourth family, a family consisting only of harmonics, of artificial resonances. In my orchestration, too, I have artificial resonances, resonances purposely added by the composer and imposed on the listener by the orchestral writing.

CLAUDE SAMUEL. So that's how your passion for the piano and your profession as organist have contributed to the formation of your orchestral language.

OLIVIER MESSIAEN. My language has a third source; it's my love for nature and birdsong. Indeed, birdsong has very varied timbre according to the species, habitat or country of the bird. Some birds even present real melodies of timbres. The song thrush, for example, will sometimes produce twenty different timbres during the course of the same phrase. That too has served me as a model.

CLAUDE SAMUEL. In examining your scores, one is struck by the variety in the orchestral constitution of your works, a constitution which is often rather strange. Here I'm thinking of certain works in which you suppress the strings . . .

OLIVIER MESSIAEN. The suppression of the strings is due to certain miscalculations. Doubtless you've noticed that our modern orchestra has become increasingly rich in wind and brass with an obviously insufficient number of strings. Let's take the case of a universally recognised masterpiece like *The Rite of Spring*: in this work (apart from passages where the strings are used alone, as in a few bars at the beginning of the second part, or when they're associated with a small group, as in the *Mysterious rounds of the young maidens* when three oboes

29

blend with three cellos) it is certain that the strings will disappear in the great fortissimo tuttis, *Spring Auguries* and *Ritual Dance*; they are completely eaten up by the brutal accents of the woodwind and brass. Here then is a lack of balance, perfectly acceptable because the work is skilfully orchestrated (with know-how), but it's nevertheless a lack of balance and it's tiresome to collect sixty to seventy instruments on a platform and not hear them.

CLAUDE SAMUEL. If you avoid the massive use of strings, you make up for it by bringing in the percussion in force.

OLIVIER MESSIAEN. That's a rather symbolic domain for our time. Like me, you've noticed the vogue for vibraphones, bells, gongs and all the instruments with prolonged resonance, explicable by the need we feel, perhaps under the influence of *musique concrète* and electronic music, to use new timbres and, above all, timbres the resonance of which produces a certain mystery. These instruments offer us power, poetry and unreality, as much the vibraphones with their vibrating resonance as the gongs, the tam-tams and the bells with their harmonic haloes, their resultants of false fundamentals and other very complex phenomena of sound which bring us close to some of the enormous and strange noises in nature like waterfalls and mountain torrents.

CLAUDE SAMUEL. Don't you think that the mysterious sensation produced by these instruments derives from the fact of their novelty? If they're used for long, they risk losing this mystery.

OLIVIER MESSIAEN. That's possible. There inevitably occurs a kind of familiarisation, but the strangeness of their resonance will still hold good. They're astonishing instruments, and always have been; those who use them in Asia and black Africa regard them as magical, and I think they're right.

CLAUDE SAMUEL. What can you tell us about new electric instruments like the Ondes Martenot?

OLIVIER MESSIAEN. I've a great affection for the Ondes Martenot, which allows for the creation of new timbres and new accents almost at will. Arthur Honegger, in *Sémiramis* and in *Joan of Arc at the Stake*, was the first composer to use them, then André

Jolivet used them in one of his youthful works, the *Danse incantatoire* for two Ondes Martenot and orchestra, and a first-rate Concerto for Ondes Martenot. I myself have used the Ondes Martenot a lot, particularly in my *Trois petites Liturgies* and *Turangalîla-Symphonie*.

CLAUDE SAMUEL. How would you define the sonority of the Ondes Martenot?

OLIVIER MESSIAEN. "Sonority" is the wrong word, since the Ondes has a great number of timbres. There is the specific timbre of the instrument which is called the *"timbre onde"*, but there are many others. One of them, much used because it contains the mystery of instruments with metallic resonance (thanks to the presence of a little gong in the diffuser), is the *"timbre métallisé"* or *"métallique"*, which produces absolutely terrifying, even harrowing effects when used loudly, and haloed with unreality when used softly. There's also a category of very interesting timbres induced by the *palm*; the *palm* is a diffuser surmounted by a little lyre, the strings of which vibrate in sympathy with the notes played. This process gives rise to sonorities that are complex, of great, even infinite delicacy . . .

CLAUDE SAMUEL. We return again to mysterious zones, the mystery which you evoke with the Ondes Martenot, which you spoke of in regard to percussion. This mystery and magic meet at every step of your progress as a creator, as when you think of colours, imagine harmonies or use instruments. How could one fail to notice how your thought is crystallised around a few ideas which constitute the very essence of your human and musical personality?

31

Conversation 3

CLAUDE SAMUEL. One day, when I said you were a composer, you added: "I'm an ornithologist and a rhythmician". In what sense should the second of these titles be understood?

OLIVIER MESSIAEN. I consider that rhythm is the primordial and perhaps essential part of music: I think it probably existed before melody and harmony, and in fact I've a secret preference for this element. I prize this preference all the more because I think it marked my entry into contemporary music.

CLAUDE SAMUEL. Before examining the details of your researches and of your rhythmic language, we could do with a little terminology so as to dispel misunderstandings. What is rhythm? How can it be defined in a simple manner?

OLIVIER MESSIAEN. Rhythm is the one musical idea which can't be defined simply. Innumerable definitions have been proposed, both good and bad according to the perspective from which they are considered. One of them—by Dom Mocquereau—is very famous and sums up the ideas of Plato and the ancient Greeks on the subject: "Rhythm is the ordering of movement". This definition has the advantage of being applicable to dancing, to words and to music, but it is incomplete.

CLAUDE SAMUEL. Let's take some concrete examples, please. What is rhythmic music?

OLIVIER MESSIAEN. Schematically, rhythmic music is music that scorns repetition, straightforwardness and equal divisions. In short, it's music inspired by the movements of nature, movements of free and unequal durations.

33

CLAUDE SAMUEL. What was the attitude of the great classical masters in regard to rhythm?

OLIVIER MESSIAEN. The classics, in the Western sense of the term, were bad rhythmicians, or, rather, composers who knew nothing of rhythm. In Bach's music there are harmonic colours, and extraordinary contrapuntal craftsmanship; it's marvellous and inspired, but there's no rhythm.

CLAUDE SAMUEL. Perhaps this statement will help us to avoid ambiguities: for some music-lovers a Bach *allegro* or a Prokofiev concerto constitutes the summit of "rhythmic music", whilst a Mozart symphony isn't at all rhythmic.

OLIVIER MESSIAEN. On the contrary, Mozart is an extraordinary rhythmician. As for the works of Bach or Prokofiev, they appear rhythmic precisely because they have no rhythm. The explanation is this: in these works an uninterrupted succession of equal note-values plunges the listener into a state of beatific satisfaction; nothing thwarts his pulse, breathing or heartbeats. Thus he is very much at ease, receives no shock, and all this appears to him to be perfectly "rhythmic".

CLAUDE SAMUEL. Let's take another example: traditional jazz is said to be "rhythmic music". . . .

OLIVIER MESSIAEN. That's exactly the same process. Jazz is established against a background of equal note-values. By the play of syncopations it also contains rhythms, but these syncopations only exist because they're placed on equal note-values which they contradict. Despite the rhythm produced by this contradiction, the listener once again settles down to the equal note-values which give him great comfort.

Here's another very striking example of non-rhythmic music which is thought rhythmic: the military march. The march, with its cadential gait and uninterrupted succession of absolutely equal note-values, is anti-natural. True marching is accompanied by an extremely irregular swaying; it's a series of falls, more or less avoided, placed at different intervals.

CLAUDE SAMUEL. Military music, then, is the negation of rhythm?

OLIVIER MESSIAEN. Absolutely.

34

CLAUDE SAMUEL. Can you give us, on the contrary, examples of strongly rhythmic music?

OLIVIER MESSIAEN. The different aspects of rhythm must be considered. First of all, the kinematics, which correspond to the definition of rhythm which I gave a moment ago, the "ordering of movement"; this concerns the alternation of impulses and rests which the Greeks so aptly called *arsis* and *thesis*. Now, all well-made music constantly includes this alternation of impulses and rests. Plainsong, to cite only one case, is an uninterrupted succession of *arsis* and *thesis*, rises and drops, of impulses and rests, as was perfectly illustrated by the greatest theoretician of plainsong, Dom Mocquereau.

CLAUDE SAMUEL. Can you also give us examples of interesting music in the rhythmic field in the Western classical repertory?

OLIVIER MESSIAEN. The greatest rhythmician in classical music is certainly Mozart. Mozartian rhythm dons a kinematic aspect, but it belongs above all to the field of accent, deriving from word and speech. With Mozart, one distinguishes between masculine and feminine groups. The first are in a single volley, coming to a dead stop, just like the male body and character; the feminine groups (more supple, like the female body and character) are the more important and characteristic, including a preparatory period called the "anacrusis", a more or less intense apex which is the "accent", and a more or less weak falling back (the "mute" or "flexional ending", formed of one or several note-values). Mozart continually used these rhythmic groups, which have so great an importance in his work that, if the exact placing of the accents is not observed, Mozartian music is completely destroyed. This is why so many bad interpretations of Mozart are heard, for most musicians are not sufficiently educated in rhythm to discern the true position of the accents.

CLAUDE SAMUEL. So the principal difficulty in playing Mozart's works lies in their rhythmic wealth?

OLIVIER MESSIAEN. Absolutely, and above all in the placing of accents, which are not always explicitly indicated by the composer; it's the melodic line, harmonic artifice, or a number of varying signs too long to enumerate which guide the

35

performer in the placing of accents. If he makes a mistake, he commits the crime of *lèse*-Mozart by completely destroying the rhythmic movement of the work.

CLAUDE SAMUEL.   Did Mozart consciously undertake this rhythmic research?

OLIVIER MESSIAEN.   Certainly. It's too consistent in his work not to have been premeditated.

CLAUDE SAMUEL.   And Beethoven?

OLIVIER MESSIAEN.   With Beethoven, rhythms and themes have a masculine appeal, and are thus in a single volley, without special accents; this is probably due to his strong and wilful character. It should be well understood that there's much less rhythmic research in Beethoven than in Mozart—the research there is on a different plane—but all the same, an interesting point is the "development by elimination" which is a sketch of the "rhythmic characters" of *The Rite of Spring*. We will perhaps revert to this . . .

CLAUDE SAMUEL.   Let's pursue our investigation among "rhythmic" composers with a compulsory stop at Debussy.

OLIVIER MESSIAEN.   We spoke of Claude Debussy in the matter of orchestration and of his love for nature, the wind and water. This love led him directly to the irregularity in note-values which I've mentioned, and which is the nature of rhythm, allowing it to avoid repetitions, at least repetitions "by return". (The repetitions in Debussy are immediate.) By dint of holding nature in check, Debussy understood its mobile aspect, and brought a perpetual undulation into his music. Because of this, he was one of the greatest rhythmicians of all time.

CLAUDE SAMUEL.   Doesn't this freedom of rhythm involve a renewal of form? Isn't there a link between the form of a work and this rhythmic treatment?

OLIVIER MESSIAEN.   I don't think so; they're two distinct fields.

CLAUDE SAMUEL.   Let's leave Debussy, then, to tackle the case of Stravinsky which you have long analysed. What is the rhythmic contribution of *The Rite of Spring*?

OLIVIER MESSIAEN.   I don't know if Stravinsky himself has realised the great innovation in *The Rite* which I've called "the

36

rhythmic characters". I'm very proud of this term, which seems really explicit to me.

CLAUDE SAMUEL. It is explicit but all the same it demands fuller explanation.

OLIVIER MESSIAEN. Very well. I spoke a moment ago of Beethoven as the creator of "development by elimination". This development consists in taking a thematic fragment and gradually taking notes away from it until it becomes entirely concentrated in an extremely short moment. Now, this elimination and its opposite, amplification—which, in other words, cause a theme to die or revive by the subtraction or addition of a certain number of note-values, as if it were dealing with a living being—constitutes the birth of the rhythmic characters, with the difference that with Beethoven only a single character is active.

In this system of rhythmic characters you have, in principle, several characters present. Let's imagine a scene in a play between three characters: the first acts in a brutal manner by hitting the second; the second character suffers this act, since his actions are dominated by those of the first; lastly, the third character is present at the conflict but remains inactive. If we transpose this parable into the field of rhythm, we have three rhythmic groups: the first, whose note-values are always increasing, is the character who attacks; the second, whose note-values decrease, is the character who is attacked; and the third, whose note-values never change, is the character who remains immobile.

CLAUDE SAMUEL. You have defined these rhythmic characters in relation to their use in *The Rite of Spring*, then you yourself have used them. What relationship of cause and effect should be distinguished between these two steps?

OLIVIER MESSIAEN. It's very difficult to explain. I know that in analysing *The Rite of Spring* I long reflected on the rhythmic importance of such passages as the *Glorification of the Chosen One* and the *Ritual Dance* and that I finished by understanding that the procedure which endowed these two pieces with all their magic power was that of the *rhythmic characters*; then I realised that this procedure had been foreshadowed by Beethoven. But I am without doubt the first to have consciously used these characters.

CLAUDE SAMUEL. At what period did you analyse *The Rite of Spring?*

OLIVIER MESSIAEN. It's very long ago. When I began to analyse *The Rite* for myself alone, I must have been twenty-two. Later, after the second war, I divulged this analysis to my pupils, to my harmony class at the Conservatoire and above all to the private composition class I held *chez* Guy Bernard-Delapierre. These classes grouped together my first and most famous pupils: Pierre Boulez, Yvonne Loriod, Yvette Grimaud, Jean-Louis Martinet, Françoise Aubut (now an organist in Quebec), Maurice Le Roux and Claud Prior (who has long been in a Swiss publishing house and is also a composer). It was a very extraordinary group, and its members chose an interesting name for it: they didn't call themselves the Messiaen pupils but "the Arrows".

CLAUDE SAMUEL. That's a very apt name . . .

OLIVIER MESSIAEN. Yes, it's very good; we thought we were projecting arrows towards the future, and when I learned that I was a Sagittarian, it gave me quite a shock!

CLAUDE SAMUEL. We will come back later to your pupils, but for the moment let's speak again of the rhythmic innovations of *The Rite of Spring.* You first revealed these innovations more than thirty years after the creation of the work. How is it that so essential an aspect of *The Rite* could have passed unnoticed for so long?

OLIVIER MESSIAEN. At the time of its creation, *The Rite* caused a terrible scandal by reason of the strangeness of its choreography to its Parisian spectators. The scandal was also provoked by the polytonal structure of the work or, rather, by its dissonant aspect, reinforced by the enormous orchestral blocks used by Stravinsky. But rhythm was relegated to second place, which is rather curious, for it was the most inspired element in Stravinsky's score, and his immediate contemporaries, even the great composers of the period, weren't interested in it.

CLAUDE SAMUEL. It could be said then that *The Rite* was a "rhythmic" work, but taking the word "rhythmic" in an inexact sense.

OLIVIER MESSIAEN. Yes, because there also exists in *The Rite*, parallel to the rhythmic characters, a concession to equal note-values; beneath the silences instigated by these characters, you can see, I dare say, wordless counterpoints made by the percussion; the superposition of rhythmic characters and these wordless counterpoints result in equal semiquavers and in this we revert to the procedure of an identical note-value interminably repeated.

CLAUDE SAMUEL. So *The Rite* represents the extremely rare case of a work which is "rhythmic" in both senses of the term?

OLIVIER MESSIAEN. Let's say that it's polyvalent, but in the last resort it is its magic power which attracts one.

CLAUDE SAMUEL. As a rhythmician you place yourself in the line of Mozart-Debussy-Stravinsky. But in order to understand your rhythmic language better it's also necessary to study two other sources which you yourself have revealed in your writings and lectures: Hindu rhythms and Greek metres.

OLIVIER MESSIAEN. I discovered Greek metres through two of my teachers: Marcel Dupré, my organ professor, who made me improvise in Greek rhythms and who spoke of them in his *Traité d'Improvisation*, and Maurice Emmanuel, my history of music professor, who gave a year's course on Greek metres which I had the luck to attend. To be sure, I gained only fragmentary information because both courses were limited in time, but this led me to study Greek metre on my own. I encountered many difficulties, first of all because I neither speak nor read Ancient Greek, and then because there are very few books on Greek metres. I had to ferret around in libraries gleaning here and there the elements of these metres, but I think that my understanding of them is now quite in focus; I have, moreover, prepared for my second treatise an enormous chapter on Greek metres which will form one of the most considerable sections of the book.

CLAUDE SAMUEL. I'm not going to ask you to summarise this

chapter in a few words, but could you nevertheless give us a general idea of the constitution of Greek metres?

OLIVIER MESSIAEN. Greek metres rely on a simple and essential principle: they are composed of shorts and longs; the shorts are all equal and a long equals two shorts. This may strike you as a self-evident truth, but it's extremely important, for, influenced by the habits of Western music, many researchers have thought they have found either bars of equal time or of irrational values in Ancient Greek rhythms, where they don't exist. In fact, they have destroyed certain relationships between the short and long values which resulted in odd numbers (like the number five for the Paeons or the number seven for the Epitrites), which resulted further to unexpected combinations such as the Dochmiac rhythms which groups an iamb with a Cretic rhythm, a triple measure and a quintuple measure, giving a total of eight short values.

Greek metres were based on a second principle whence comes the word "metric": poetry, music and dance, which were closely linked, relied on metre. Metre is quite simply the grouping of two feet, the foot being a rhythm composed of a certain number of short and long values each having a precise name. In a succession of like feet, "substitutes" can be used. Take an iambic verse with its continual short-long, short-long, short-long, etc. One has the right to effect substitutions, that is to say that a short-long rhythm may be replaced by its equivalent value, the tribrach (three short values) or one may further substitute for this ensemble, forming groups of three, a rhythm which gives groups of four, for example a dactyl (long-short-short). Very often the last foot of a verse, normally ternary, is a quadruplet, made up of a spondee which groups two longs (equal to four shorts). This play of substitutions may, by adding up all the note-values of a verse, result in unexpected numbers, among others prime numbers. You may thus obtain the number eleven in Aristophanian verse (with a spondee substituted for the last foot)—or the number seventeen in minor Sapphic verse (with a spondee substituted for the last foot). These primary numbers are quite unused in classical Western music.

40

CLAUDE SAMUEL. So it's a greater refinement.

OLIVIER MESSIAEN. Yes, but, outside this important process of substitution, we have metres and feet based exclusively on odd and on primary numbers. Among the rhythms based on the number five, we find all the series of Paeons, and the extraordinary Cretic rhythm which the Greeks borrowed from the Cretans. We'll revert later to this Cretic rhythm (long-short-long) which is non-retrogradable. Permutations of the Cretic rhythm give the Bacchius (short-long-long) and the Antibacchius (long-long-short), always in a quintuple time. Then there are the rhythms in seven, the Epitrites, comprising three longs and a short, the placing of which is variable. Another peculiarity of Greek metre is Logaoedic verse. These verses combine three and fours, that is to say, they don't present a foot type but comprise fours, such as the dactyl, and threes, like the trochee, mixed. The poets Alcaeus of Mytilene, Asclepius of Athens and the poetess Sappho particularly used these verses and grouped them in famous strophes, called "Alcaic", "Asclepiadean" and "Sapphic".

Beyond these main elements of Greek metre may be noticed a few innovatory details. I discovered one of them when analysing Claude Le Jeune's *Le Printemps*, one of the most beautiful monuments to rhythm in all musical history, composed on an admirable poem by Antoine de Baïf. Le Jeune and Baïf tried to resuscitate Greek metres; the choruses of *Le Printemps* use Greek rhythms almost exclusively, mainly the minor Ionic, that is to say, a rhythm in six (two shorts and two longs). Now, the interesting point about this metre is the presence of the anaclasis; the anaclasis—remember the work by Penderecki called *Anaclasis*—consists in permutating the shorts and the longs in a rhythm, not during its course but at the intersection of the two rhythms. Let's imagine, for example, a minor Ionic trimeter (that is to say three Ionic minors). The end of the second Ionic minor and the beginning of the third are interchanged, so that you only hear the true Ionic minor at the beginning of the verse, and the result will be: Ionic minor, Paeon III, Epitrite II; that is: two shorts and two longs—then two shorts, a long and a

41

short—finally, a long, a short and two longs. The anaclasis creates a disturbance in the sequence of durations which upsets the listener. It's really a very "modern" structure which reminds one of an infernal machine imposed on peaceful rhythms. These are the salient features of Greek metres which I got to know, I repeat, not only by studying the strophes of Sophocles and Aeschylus, the odes of Pindar and the poems of Sappho, but equally from analysing *Le Printemps* of Claude Le Jeune, despite the difficulties of an analysis which I had to begin again several times and on which I am still working.

CLAUDE SAMUEL. How do you explain the fact that Western composers have neglected Greek metres when Greek culture forms an integral part of our civilisation?

OLIVIER MESSIAEN. It is rather surprising. As the preface to *Le Printemps* explains so well, Greek metres were lost for a long time. Actually, the flexibility of the neumes of plainsong, the use of *arsis* and *thesis* and the blend of twos and threes in plainsong correspond in a certain sense to a survival of Greek metres, but it required the spirit of the Renaissance and the return to antiquity to think of reverting to these rhythms. And poor Baïf and poor Le Jeune, despite their genius, were criticised by their contemporaries and even more by their successors.

CLAUDE SAMUEL. Then all this was completely forgotten . . .

OLIVIER MESSIAEN. Yes, a definitive anathema was cast on Le Jeune's *Printemps*; yet I can assure you that it's one of the greatest masterpieces in all musical history.

CLAUDE SAMUEL. Let's leave *Le Printemps* and its Greek resonances to take up another chapter: that of the Hindu sources of your rhythmic language.

OLIVIER MESSIAEN. Indian rhythms carry the names of "deçî-tâlas", from *tâla* (rhythm) and *deçî* (regional rhythm); that is to say, deçî-tâlas signify "rhythms from the different regions". We know these extremely ancient rhythms from a thirteenth-century treatise written by Çârngadeva, a compilation from several earlier collections of which some have disappeared. The deçî-tâlas cited by Çârngadeva in the *Sangîta-ratnâkara*, a work whose pretentious title means "Ocean of Music", number a hundred and twenty: this number may seem enormous, but it's very small in relation to the quantity of Indian rhythms that have been lost by reason of the fact that they were transmitted by an oral tradition. Thus today we possess books containing long lists of the names of rhythms, but these names are only symbols for something no longer known.

CLAUDE SAMUEL.   Have the Indian deçî-tâlas fallen into disuse?

OLIVIER MESSIAEN.   I think they're still used by certain Brahmins and by certain other castes, but the Hindu music to be heard today, despite the virtuosity of its râgas, the beauty of its symbols, its modes and its rhythms, is rather far from the hundred and twenty deçî-tâlas which I just mentioned, deçî-tâlas which represent without a doubt the summit of Hindu and human rhythmic creation!

I have long studied the hundred and twenty deçî-tâlas which were assembled in some disorder by Çârngadeva: so long that I ended by discovering the different rhythmic rules which they unfold, as well as the religious, philosophical and cosmic symbols contained in them. It would take too long to explain all these symbols, which I've collected in a book, but I can give you the general rules engendered by these rhythms. These are: the principle of the addition of a dot; the principle of the increasing and decreasing of one value in two; the principle of inexact augmentation; and that of dissociation and coagulation. The primordial element is the existence of special rhythms which I have termed "non-retrogradable".

A non-retrogradable rhythm is quite simply a grouping of values which read identically from left to right or from right to left, that is to say, which present exactly the same successive order of values, read in either direction. The simplest are, for example, the non-retrogradable rhythms of three values—the outer durations being identical and the central duration free. Equally, all rhythms divisible into two groups which are retrograde in relation to each other, having a common central value, are non-retrogradable. It's as if in traversing a landscape, beginning from two opposite points, you were to meet the same

43

things at the same times in the same positions and in the same order.

It's extraordinary to think that the Hindus were the first to point out and use—rhythmically and musically—this principle of non-retrogradation which is so often encountered around us. It's a principle which has long been applied to architecture: thus in ancient art, gothic and romanesque cathedrals and even in modern art, the decorative figures ornamenting the pediments of the portals are nearly always two symmetrically inverse figures framing a neutral central motif. Ancient magical formulae included words which had, it appears, an occult power. It was impossible to read these words from left to right, then from right to left, without meeting exactly the same sound and the same order of letters. In nature we have an exquisite example: the wings of a butterfly. When butterflies are enclosed in their chrysalis, their wings are folded and stuck one against the other; the pattern on one is thus reproduced in the opposite direction on the other. Later, when the wings unfold, there will be a pattern with colours on the right wing which mirror those on the left, and the body of the butterfly, the thorax and the antennae placed between the two wings constitute the central value. These are marvellous living non-retrogradable rhythms.

Finally, we carry these rhythms in ourselves. Our face with its two symmetrical eyes, its two symmetrical ears, and the nose in the middle; our opposite hands with their opposed thumbs, our two arms, and the central thorax; and the tree of its nervous system with all its symmetrical branchings. These are non-retrogradable rhythms. A final symbol: this moment which I live, this thought which crosses my mind, this movement which I accomplish, this time which I beat: before it and after it lies eternity: it's a non-retrogradable rhythm.

CLAUDE SAMUEL. These examples clearly indicate the significance you attach to non-retrogradable rhythms. Let's speak now of your own experiment in Hindu rhythms. How did you come to have the idea of exploring this universe that is so foreign to our Western feelings and preoccupations?

OLIVIER MESSIAEN. It was by a stroke of luck. I came across the treatise of Çârngadeva and the famous list of a hundred and twenty deçî-talas; this list was a revelation, I immediately felt that this was an extraordinary mine. I looked at it, copied it, contemplated and went back to it in every sense for years in order to arrive at a grasp of its hidden meaning.

CLAUDE SAMUEL. Were these texts published in French?

OLIVIER MESSIAEN. No, and at the time I didn't understand Sanskrit words. By another lucky chance, a Hindu friend translated the text for me, which allowed me to discover beyond the rhythmic rules the cosmic and religious symbols contained in each deçî-tâla. Thus, most of the rhythms based on the numbers five or fifteen (three times five) are dedicated to Shiva; they are also dedicated to Pârvati: wife, shakti and the power of Shiva's manifestation.

CLAUDE SAMUEL. Is it also possible to discover symbols in your own rhythm?

OLIVIER MESSIAEN. No. I've used Hindu rhythms and rhythmic principles a great deal, but when I used them, I still didn't know the meaning of the Sanskrit words, and so I was unaware of the symbols. Yet I often approached them unconsciously. There's a rhythm called Gajalîla, a rhythm of the elephant play, composed of three quavers and a dotted fourth quaver, which gives a kind of heaviness and limp which goes well with the symbol of the elephant play, a symbol dear to the Hindus. For us, an elephant which amuses itself by jumping over a rope is rather funny, but this isn't at all the case for Hindus, who depict the world as four elephants resting on four tortoises, which rest on nothing. The number of the elephant-god, Ganesha, is also four. Gajalîla has four note-values, and the fourth, which is dotted, depicts perhaps the mental crank. I don't want to give you other explanations, for there's a real theology of illusion against reality and of reality against illusion, but it's curious to realise that I've always used the Gajalîla rhythm in this sense; so it's necessary to believe that this grouping of note-values contains a magic formula . . .

CLAUDE SAMUEL. Here's magic again . . . Isn't the interest you take in Hindu rhythms partly due to the attraction of the mysterious and magical?

OLIVIER MESSIAEN. If you wish, in the best sense of the term: in the sense of a hidden ritual the signs of which are only revealed to the initiated. I don't think that this is forbidden by the Church and by religion; it's an admirable thing which has no connection with black magic and devilry.

CLAUDE SAMUEL. Has India other charms for you?

OLIVIER MESSIAEN. No, I'm interested above all in rhythm. In order to understand rhythm and symbols better, I've obviously read works on religions, philosophies and Hindu religious theories, which are quite remarkable; but nevertheless I haven't been converted to Buddhism, Hinduism or to Shivaism.

CLAUDE SAMUEL. Do you know of other Western composers who have had knowledge of Hindu rhythms?

OLIVIER MESSIAEN. No, I'm absolutely alone in this. But I remember the labours in France of Alain Daniélou, who lived a long time in India and who has written several books on India, in particular on the divisions of the octave and the "shrutis" in the Hindu modes, and on Indian philosophies, religions and Hindu polytheism.

CLAUDE SAMUEL. Do you teach this Hindu rhythm to your pupils?

OLIVIER MESSIAEN. I've often spoken of it and I've even given special courses in Greek metres and Hindu rhythm at Darmstadt, Tanglewood, Sarrebrücken, Budapest, and quite recently in Buenos Aires, for students coming from all the South and Central American states.

CLAUDE SAMUEL. But now that, thanks to you, these hundred and twenty Indian deçî-tâlas have been revealed, do you think that composers will use them?

OLIVIER MESSIAEN. That's already happened! But they don't think of India, they take some rhythmic formulae from my music and so use deçî-tâlas without knowing it.

CLAUDE SAMUEL. Would your rhythms have been very different if you hadn't known about deçî-tâlas?

OLIVIER MESSIAEN. I can't answer that. In any case, I was directed towards these discoveries, towards asymmetric divisions and towards an element which I met in Greek metres and Indian rhythms: the prime numbers. Even as a child I loved prime numbers, these numbers which, by the simple fact of not being divisible into equal fractions, emitted an occult power (for you know that divinity is not divisible ...)

CLAUDE SAMUEL. Yet another mystery ...

OLIVIER MESSIAEN. Yes, yet another mystery, and so great a mystery that the most experienced mathematicians have never been able to explain the placing of prime numbers in the infinite unfolding of whole numbers.

CLAUDE SAMUEL. After having characterised these different elements, could you place your own rhythmic language?

OLIVIER MESSIAEN. My rhythmic language is precisely a mixture of all these elements; the note-values distributed in irregular numbers, the absence of equal times and symmetrical bars, the love of prime numbers, the presence of some non-retrogradable rhythms and the action of rhythmic characters. All this is contained in my rhythmic language; all this evolves, is blended and superimposed in it.

CLAUDE SAMUEL. Does the use of this language imply a conscious step or a spontaneous reflex?

OLIVIER MESSIAEN. Both.

CLAUDE SAMUEL. Which of your works are the most representative of your rhythmic preoccupations?

OLIVIER MESSIAEN. Nearly all of them, especially my *Quatre Etudes de rythme* for piano, the *Turangalîla-Symphonie*, the *Livre d'Orgue* and *Chronochromie* (the peculiarity of which is that it contains "symmetrical permutations" always inverted in the same order of reading).

CLAUDE SAMUEL. Has your rhythmic language been modified throughout your evolution?

OLIVIER MESSIAEN. Yes, notably in my recent works; in them I've included irrational values, which didn't interest me much formerly but which the young composers use a great deal, as well as a new concept of tempo according to which, in a given rhythm, you can change, not its progress, but its quality, by transforming it in *accelerando* or *rallentando*.

CLAUDE SAMUEL. Could you also tell us about the rhythmic language of the young composers to whom you have transmitted your theories?

OLIVIER MESSIAEN. Pierre Boulez was the most influenced by my rhythmic discoveries; nevertheless, his approach is different from mine and, above all, he had the intelligence to associate himself with the serial procedures of Webern and the system of irrational note-values which, beginning with Chopin, were pursued by Debussy and found one of their best expressions in the works of Varèse and Jolivet. It's certain that Boulez has collected, transformed and digested all this, then he has added his own honey, but in the end he is still my heir. However it must be recognised that he has gone beyond all of us!

I will next cite the research into irrational values carried to its extreme by Karlheinz Stockhausen: there are in his *Klavierstücke* I to IV and in his *Zeitmasse* irrational values of extreme complexity which have caused rhythm to progress.

We have actually arrived at these great areas of long durations which extend beyond not only classical rhythms but even Greek metre, the deçî-tâlas of India and irrational values. We are witnessing a change in the notion of time and I believe that one of the young composers for whom this change is most perceptible is Jean-Claude Eloy. Beyond the refinement of timbre and the quality of "heterophony", I discern in Jean-Claude Eloy's music a concept of time that is quite at the spearhead of the avant-garde.

CLAUDE SAMUEL. But what place do you attribute to these rhythmic discoveries in the musical evolution of the time?

OLIVIER MESSIAEN. It's probably the most important characteristic of twentieth-century music, and that which distinguishes our epoch from previous centuries.

CLAUDE SAMUEL. Don't these innovations lead to musical scores that are extremely difficult to grasp at a first reading and very difficult to interpret without some inaccuracy?

OLIVIER MESSIAEN. That doesn't worry me. Remember the

48

example of past centuries: in the nineteenth century, no one could perform the Studies of Chopin apart from Liszt and Chopin himself; now all good pianists play them. Fifty years ago, the *Préludes* of Debussy were considered not only unplayable but unreadable; everyone spoke of "distorted harmonies", reproached the great number of accidentals ... what accusations were *not* levelled against Debussy! Today it seems so simple. For players, as for listeners, there is here the phenomenon of familiarisation.

CLAUDE SAMUEL. And the listener, how should he take to this rhythmic research? Should he be responsive to it on hearing it, or test it by reading it?

OLIVIER MESSIAEN. He'll be responsive to it the day his ear becomes accustomed to it. It isn't essential that the listener should be able to judge precisely all the rhythmic procedures of the music he hears, any more than he has need to figure all the chords of classical music. That's reserved for harmony teachers and professional composers ... The moment he receives a shock, that it's lovely, that the music moves him, the aim is achieved!

BIRDSONG

Conversation 4

CLAUDE SAMUEL. Oliver Messiaen, as soon as you hear the word "bird", your face lights up; this isn't only the reaction of a composer, it's also a human reaction, for, if birds occupy so great a place in your musical language, this is first of all because you're a nature-lover.

OLIVIER MESSIAEN. Certainly. It's probable that in the artistic hierarchy birds are the greatest musicians existing on our planet. Moreover, from all points of view the bird is a marvellous creature: flight is still an unexplored marvel. Migration is another marvel which has caused rivers of ink to flow, and of which one of its greatest specialists, M. Jean Dorst, is obliged to recognise that our knowledge is still incomplete; and what about the triple vision of most birds (monocular vision on the right and left, binocular in front) which allows them to fly away from danger, to explore a countryside and to mark down their prey at the same time! But the greatest of all these marvels, the most precious for a composer of music, is obviously birdsong.

Strange though this may seem, birdsong has first of all a territorial aspect; a bird sings to defend its branch, its field of pasture, and to affirm his ownership of a female, a nest, or a branch, of a region in which he lives and feeds; it's also true that the differences between birds on the subject of possession of a territory are often regulated by song contests, and if the predator improperly wishes to occupy a spot which doesn't belong to it, the true owner sings and sings so well that the predator goes away . . .

CLAUDE SAMUEL. It's the second Act of *Tannhäuser!*

51

OLIVIER MESSIAEN. Yes, but there's also an upsetting of the situation which Wagner didn't foresee: if the robber sings better than the true proprietor, the proprietor yields his place. If only we could regulate the many differences between human beings in this charming manner ...

The second reason for birdsong is obviously the amorous impulse, and this is why birds sing above all in springtime, the time of love. Birdsong is, in principle—apart from a few rare exceptions—the prerogative of the male, who sings to attract the female. Other amorous manifestations—nuptial parades, showing off the beauties of plumage or qualities of flight—are also designed to dazzle the female. The love-songs are among the most beautiful. But there is a third category of birdsong, which is quite admirable and which I place above all the others: that is free song, without social function and generally provoked by the beauties of dawning or dying light. Thus, I've noticed in the Jura an especially gifted Song Thrush, the song of which was absolutely inspired when the sunset was very beautiful with magnificent red and violet lighting. When the colours were less beautiful or when the sunset was shorter, this thrush didn't sing, or sang less interesting themes.

Finally, one must speak of the musical sounds emitted by birds which professional ornithologists classify not as "songs" but as "calls". These birdcalls constitute a true musical language, and here we join up with the affecting discovery of Wagner, who really strove to express ideas in musical code by means of the *leitmotiv*. Indeed, birds converse in calls with precise meanings quite easy to recognise; there are, for example, the call to love, the call to food, the cry of alarm. The cry of alarm is so important that, whatever the species emitting it to call attention to an imminent danger, all birds understand it.

To summarise, then, the different categories of vocal emissions by birds: on the one hand the means of communicating with society (that is to say the calls); on the other hand the songs, properly speaking (which may be territorial, seductive or, the most beautiful of all, the free song which salutes the dawning or dying light).

CLAUDE SAMUEL. But there is also a very great diversity in birdsong according to the species, the regions . . .

OLIVIER MESSIAEN. Yes indeed, the difference is considerable according to the species; first of all among the species of the same country, then among the species of the same habitat and finally among the same species in the world.

CLAUDE SAMUEL. How many species of bird are there?

OLIVIER MESSIAEN. About twelve thousand, and every one has its own specific song.

CLAUDE SAMUEL. How many species have you studied?

OLIVIER MESSIAEN. I honestly don't know, but I can recognise by ear and without hesitation the songs of fifty species in France. For some five hundred and fifty other species living in France and Europe, I need a moment's reflection, sometimes recourse to a manual or to watch with binoculars, or to have supplementary information as to the behaviour, habitat, and so on . . . Among the foreign species, I know well some North American birds but less well those of South America, because countries like Brazil and the Amazon forest are little known (birds are even found there which are not yet catalogued!). Finally, I know well the birds of Japan, thanks to a recent tour. This seems a lot, but it's minimal in comparison with the total number of birds in the world. I know other birdsong from records, mainly that of New Zealand and Australia, but as I've never been to these countries, I daren't say that I have a true knowledge of them.

I told you that each species has its own specific song. There again one may distinguish several categories. First, the birds that have an innate song, that is to say that they are born with a certain style and aesthetic, and, as soon as one hears them, one says right away, "That's a blackbird! That's a thrush! That's a nightingale!", just as at a concert of classical music you can say, "That's Mozart! That's Debussy! That's Berlioz!"

On the other hand, some birds haven't this innate song and are obliged to learn it rather painfully from their parents. A very common and virtuosic bird, the finch, has no innate song; young finches work under the direction of their father and generally have much difficulty in arriving at the end of the victorious roulade they compose. It must be acknowledged that it's a difficult song to sing, containing repeated notes, then a roll, slow at first but accelerating wildly and getting louder and louder. This accelerando ends in a victorious codetta, which may descend or ascend, following the regional and dialectal endings. It's extremely difficult to get right and the young finches may be heard stumbling over the final notes without being able to bring off this rare coda.

The resemblances between one species and another should also be pointed out; thus the Willow Warbler also has an accelerando on a rolled note, but, instead of having the victorious codetta of the finch, it has a dying fall, slowing and sad, and above all it doesn't learn only a single codetta but ceaselessly invents new ones.

CLAUDE SAMUEL.   And to think that we ingenuously thought that each bird had a short and always identical song!

OLIVIER MESSIAEN.   That's untrue! The song depends on the species and also on the characteristic of the individual, for at the heart of the same species there are always variants between the individuals. I'll give you a few examples. First of all, a bird known by everyone: the blackbird, the famous black bird with a yellow beak, which is met with not only in the country but today also in the gardens of our towns. The blackbird has an aesthetic characteristic of formulae reverting to a high-pitch; its song, both solemn and bantering, is based, if not on a hyper-major mode, at least on the use of the major third, perfect fourth and major sixth and augmented fourth. Every spring each blackbird invents a certain number of themes which it retains and which it adds to previous themes; the older it gets, the vaster its repertory of melodic motifs becomes, and these motifs are peculiar to each individual bird.

Let's speak now of another very well-known bird which is never seen but is heard a lot in springtime, by day and night: the nightingale, which all poets have extolled . . .

CLAUDE SAMUEL.   Is it true that the nightingale sings better than any other bird?

OLIVIER MESSIAEN. No, that isn't true. The nightingale is a great tenor, with a very powerful voice, the virtuosity of which is remarkable. (Let's open a parenthesis: birds have extraordinary virtuosity which no tenor or coloratura soprano could ever equal, for they possess a peculiar vocal organ, a "syrinx" which allows them to perform rolls and very small intervals, and to sing extremely fast. This virtuosity reminds me of a little anecdote: some years ago, Manuel Rosenthal's wife, who is a singer and singing-teacher, had bought a superb Indian *shama* (a marvellous singing cage-bird); the *shama* sang all day long, and during lessons, excited by music in the next room, it redoubled its efforts, singing so well that the pupils were ashamed of their own voices: finally lessons couldn't be given because so much time was spent in listening to the bird and going into ecstasies over the brilliance of its talents. . . .)
To return to the nightingale: it has a formidable virtuosity and a very powerful voice, but it's more of an actor than a singer. Nightingales have stereotyped formulae, the same for each bird, two of which are well known: an oscillation of two disjunct sounds which can be transcribed: "tiko-tiko-tiko-tiko" or "couti-couti-couti-couti"; the other is a lunar sound, very distant and very slow, which one thinks is being emitted by another bird five hundred metres away which gradually draws nearer; then this sound is brusquely followed by two or three very loud notes reverting to a high pitch. Most nightingales alternate five or six themes common to each with reversals of intensity and feelings. The nightingale performs a *volte face* of sadness to joy . . .
CLAUDE SAMUEL. What we call "sadness" . . .
OLIVIER MESSIAEN. Yes, you must excuse my using human terms, it's an old fault: I'm becoming anthropomorphic despite myself. Let's say that the nightingale appears to be passing brusquely from sadness to joy, from anger to renunciation, from rancour to forgiveness and from supplication to victory. And he really goes from a slow tempo into a rapid one, from a pianissimo nuance to a fortissimo with brusque and obvious contrasts.

I now arrive at the birds that seem greater artists to me. In France, I see two that are brilliantly gifted, the song thrush and the skylark. The skylark is a very common bird that lives in cereal-growing districts like the Champagne or the Beaune, where it makes its nest on the bare earth in a depression sheltered by a tuft of grass or a mound. It's a bird of the mid-air, yet it sleeps on the ground, which is extraordinary!

To know the song of the skylark, one must have heard thousands of them for hours, days, months and years; so you will understand that a record is an incomplete tool, for it only gives us a portion of a song, just as a photograph gives only a "snap-shot" of an individual. The skylark, this typically French bird (so typical that the Gauls took it as an emblem) sings in mid-air while flying. It's flight includes: the quasi-vertical ascent, the beatings of the wings (flapping flight), short stops in mid-air (gliding flight), and nose-dive, with closed wings, the bird recovering itself some distance from the ground in order to land gently. Its song, divided between a high note and a low one, follows these phases. It comes constantly to beat against this high note which serves as a ceiling with swift motifs always returning to the high note, like the *climacus resupinus* of plainsong, and, in the brief moments of gliding flight, the song descends to the lower register with long notes. So the song of the skylark evolves between these two extremes, the long notes of the floor and the crest of the ceiling, the remainder being garland and arabesque. The total song is swift, extremely jubilatory and alleluia-like. Only a musician could arrive at understanding it and noting it down; indeed, most ornithologists stop at its description and say "extraordinary song, impossible to describe".

Finally, the Song Thrush is one of the most inspired birds and, although each bird has its own invention, the song is nevertheless quite recognisable; it's a song of incantatory nature with strophes generally thrice repeated. But, wait! These strophes are never the same, that is to say, the bird invents a strophe, repeats it three times, then it invents another which it also repeats three times, and then the next day it'll invent a

56

dozen, each of which it'll repeat three times, but, after the three repetitions, it's over: the thrush invents a new strophe, repeated in its turn. Moreover, within these strophes, the rhythms are extremely marked and varied, and accompanied by melodies of timbres; at the heart of a rhythm, you'll often find two or three timbres. Further, between the repetitions, there are quite extraordinary flights of virtuosity, for example, water-drop glissandi in which are heard a succession of very delicate sounds, like pearls showering off a broken string or water-drops spraying into a fountain; one also hears little grating sounds, staccato sounds and light pulsations. It's all extremely varied and complex, but of great power thanks to rhythms and the three repetitions.

CLAUDE SAMUEL. Can a map be outlined of the big bird families? In other words, is it possible to discover differences between the birdsong of like species living in very distant countries?

OLIVIER MESSIAEN. Certain species have a specific song with the same aesthetic at the heart of the same continent but with dialectal variations. Thus, the Orphean Warbler of the Pyrénées-Orientales, to be heard in the cork-oaks below Banyuls, doesn't sing like the Orphean Warbler of Greece.

CLAUDE SAMUEL. Yet both belong to the same species?

OLIVIER MESSIAEN. Yes, but the song of the Greek Orphean Warbler is much more brilliant and varied than that of the French. On the other hand, there's no comparison possible between the different European warblers and the multitude of birds which the Americans call "warblers", which aren't warblers. I can also tell you that most of the birds I studied in Japan haven't their equivalents in France, even when they have a similar name. Thus the Japanese Warbler called *Uguisu* has a French namesake, a Cetti's Warbler, which is generally found in thick bramble bushes, by the water's edge in the Camargue, in Brière, and Charente. The song of this French Warbler is a very typical melodic and rhythmic formula: three separated notes of which the second is lower and shorter (the neume *porrectus*, Cretic rhythm) followed by a roll and a conclusion, the whole being very loud and brusque, seeming to

57

express a certain irritation. The song of the Japanese Warbler is quite different; it's very characteristic and recognisable' in a thousand: it's a very long note, pianissimo-crescendo, with an extremely gradual swelling which ends in a victorious *torculus* fortissimo. I've used this song and you'd recognise it very easily because it's played at least twenty times by a trumpet and a tutti of winds in *Les Oiseaux de Karuizawas* in my *Sept Haïkaï*.

CLAUDE SAMUEL. Are there mixtures of birdsong? Can birds be influenced by the song of another species?

OLIVIER MESSIAEN. Certain birds specialise in fraudulent imitation, but it's really an absolutely extraordinary faking which is more a recasting. I'll cite, for example, two exceptional birds, the Melodious Warbler of the south-west and the south of France (also to be found in Spain and Italy) and the Icterine Warbler of the French north-east (also to be found in Belgium and Switzerland). These birds, commonly called "counterfeiters", reproduce the song of others; they do so by mixings and volte-faces and a virtuosity so astounding that analysis is to all intents and purposes impossible. It's only with a record and a recording played slowly that the imitations can be revealed. I can't explain it but it's as if one was hearing Debussy re-written by Stockhausen ...

CLAUDE SAMUEL. And the migratory birds, don't they have songs that are modified according to their journeys?

OLIVIER MESSIAEN. No, migration has no connection with birdsong. In France, we have essentially migratory birds like the Golden Oriole coming directly from Africa. Its song is a strange, slurred whistling, full of a colourful joy, rich in harmonics and sunny resources. It reaches France in the springtime, at the time that it sings, then it leaves again for Africa, flying by way of Greece and Egypt to reach Kenya and Uganda, where its winter quarters are and where it doesn't sing, and consequently there's no change from one continent to another.

CLAUDE SAMUEL. After this fine lesson in ornithology, I'd like to ask you a question: how did you become an ornithologist?

OLIVIER MESSIAEN. Quite simply because I loved birdsong, and have done since my childhood; I'd noted a great number of birdsongs, very badly at first, without being able to identify the bird that was singing. I was deeply mortified by my ignorance and I asked advice from some professional ornithologists. The first person to inform me was an ornithologist and writer of great talent, now dead, called Jacques Delamain; it was on his estate in Charentes, la Branderaie de Gardépée, that I had my first lessons in ornithology; then I worked in the Camargue with Jacques Penot, on the Ile d'Ouessant with Robert-Daniel Etchecopar (who's Director of a section of the Museum of Natural History), then in the stony, sun-drenched hills of Hérault and the district of Pézenas with François Huë, and lastly and above all I went on directed outings with Henri Lomont in the region of the Pyrénées-Orientales, chiefly around Banyuls and Port-Vendres. For the rest, in France as abroad, I've worked on my own, and I can cite my notations of birdsong in the Dauphiné, in Savoy, in the Jura, the Causes, Provence and the Vivarais, in flat country like the districts of Bourges and Chartres, and I'm particularly proud of my collection of the songs of the pond birds; I've spent many hours in the Camargue, above all at Sologne noting the Reed Warbler, the Sedge Warbler, the Water Rail, the Great Reed Warbler, and all the birds of the reeds, ponds and marshes. It's to them that I've dedicated what I think to be my greatest success in birdsong: the *Rousserolle effarvarte* of my *Catalogue d'Oiseaux*; it's an enormous piece, which lasts about half an hour, the form of which is entirely based on birdsong in the reeds and ponds as the hours of the day and night unfold. In fact, the piece begins at three o'clock in the morning and finishes at three o'clock in the morning with all the intermediary hours, obviously compressed, including the intervals of silence, also condensed.

CLAUDE SAMUEL.   Could you tell us how you go about collecting birdsong?

OLIVIER MESSIAEN.   The best time is spring, the season of courtship, that is to say the months of April, May and June; and the best hours correspond to the rising and setting of the sun, that is to say the morning around six o'clock in April or between four and five in June and, for sunset, towards seven in the evening in April, around nine and even half past nine in June.

CLAUDE SAMUEL.   There's no chance of hearing birds in the middle of the day . . .

OLIVIER MESSIAEN.   But yes; some birds like the Blackcap sing in the morning and afternoon, but there's one hour during which one hears absolutely nothing: this is between noon and one o'clock.

CLAUDE SAMUEL.   That's the siesta . . .

OLIVIER MESSIAEN.   Yes, it's a moment of heat and sleepiness and everyone's silent. To this, one must add the rôle of the seasons: summer is a time of silence because the birds are parents and are occupied with feeding their young; this is a terrible task, the males are exhausted by the search for prey which must be constantly brought to the ever-open little beaks, which always complain because they're always hungry; they haven't time to sing, material cares prevail over art . . .

Then comes winter: for some it's acceptance of a very cruel cold, sometimes death, for others it's migration with formidable journeys, ranging amazingly and inexplicably over thousands of miles; no one sings any longer. There remains the autumn. when a few birds sing again: they're rather rare. In our provinces there's a bird that sings almost as much in the autumn as in the spring: the robin, quite common in France and well-known in England.

CLAUDE SAMUEL.   To be a composer-ornithologist, I suppose two qualities are indispensable: patience and an extremely practised ear . . .

OLIVIER MESSIAEN.   Yes, one must have an extremely practised ear and be capable of writing down very quickly something which is retained while listening to something else which must also be retained; so it's a matter of a rather tiring double cerebral task. I go into the country with manuscript paper, a sketch-board for support, paper-clips to hold the paper in case the wind carries it off, because one must think of everything, an army of pencils, rubbers and pencil-sharpeners . . .

CLAUDF SAMUEL.   No tape-recorder?

OLIVIER MESSIAEN. Never a tape-recorder, but a pair of field-glasses which allows me, whether out at sea or on a mountain, to distinguish from a distance the individual that is singing. Lastly I carry a little pocket manual with drawings and maps, all that could help me in cases of doubt to identify the bird.
CLAUDE SAMUEL. Try now to forget your approach as an ornithologist to explain to us your attitude as a composer. How do you make the transition between collecting to composition?
OLIVIER MESSIAEN. I've made use of birdsong in two different ways: by trying to outline the most exact musical portrait possible, or, on the other hand, by treating the birdsong as malleable material (think of the electronic manipulations in which present-day seekers indulge). To illustrate the first case, I would cite my *Catalogue d'Oiseaux* for piano, in which I've tried to depict exactly the typical birdsong of a district, surrounded by its neighbours, as well as the singing at different hours of the day and night, accompanied in the harmonic and rhythmic material by the perfumes and colours of the landscape in which the bird dwells. Personally, I'm very proud of the exactitude of my work; perhaps I'm mistaken, because people who really know the birds might not be able to recognise them in my music, and yet I will guarantee that all is accurate: but, obviously, it's I who listen and unintentionally I may introduce something of my manner of listening in reproducing the birdsong. However, I must all the same get certain combinations. I'll explain: it happens that one hears a soloist and behind it quantities of other birds that are its neighbours. The ensemble may constitute counterpoint of thirty or forty simultaneous parts! Well, in the passage called *Epôde* in my *Chronochromie* for large orchestra, there's counterpoint in eighteen simultaneous voices, all in different aesthetics, rhythms and modes. It's obvious that I didn't note these eighteen voices in one go: I noted, for example, a blackbird, but I know that at the same time a chaffinch, a Garden Warbler and a nightingale were singing; I indicated this in my notes and noted very exactly the song of this blackbird, then the next day I returned to the same place to note down the chaffinch and the

61

Garden Warbler only, the following day I noted the nightingale and so on. Finally, after the event, I combine these five, ten or twenty birdsongs. So you see that the combination is probable even if it isn't exactly what I heard.

CLAUDE SAMUEL. But isn't the main difficulty of your approach the reproduction of the timbre of the birdsong?

OLIVIER MESSIAEN. Yes, it's the major problem. But it's also one of the sources of the coloration of my orchestration for, in order to translate these timbres, harmonic combinations are absolutely necessary; now, even in very fast movements, when I reproduce birdsong, whether on the orchestra or on the piano, each note is provided with a chord, not a listed chord but a complex of sounds intended to give the timbre of this note. So many notes, so many invented chords; that's to say, for a bird piece comprising one or two thousand notes, one or two thousand invented chords. It's an enormous imaginative task.

CLAUDE SAMUEL. You try, then, less to "photograph" a "landscape" of birds than to transpose it.

OLIVIER MESSIAEN. I should also have pointed out other modifications. A bird, being much smaller than us, with a heart which beats faster and nervous reactions that are much quicker, sings in extremely brisk tempi, absolutely impossible for our instruments; so I'm obliged to transcribe the birdsong into a slower tempo. Moreover, this speed is linked to an extremely high pitch, the bird being able to sing in extremely high registers, inaccessible to our instruments; so I write one, two, three or even four octaves lower. And that's not all: for the same reasons I'm obliged to suppress very small intervals which our instruments can't play. I replace these intervals, which are of the order of one or two commas by semitones, but I respect the scale of values between the different intervals, that's to say that if a few commas correspond to a semitone, a real semitone will correspond to a whole tone or a third; all is enlarged but the relationships remain identical and, in consequence, what I restore is nevertheless exact. It's a transposition into a more human scale than that which I heard.

CLAUDE SAMUEL. Your care for accuracy astonishes me; I find

once again the preoccupation of a man of science rather than the care of a composer who might consider birdsong as a simple material delivered up to his imagination.

OLIVIER MESSIAEN. I've adopted both attitudes; I've written "exact" and "probable" pieces, the form of which respects the succession of song and silence during the hours of day and night. But I've also made use of birdsong as a material in some of my pieces like the *Couleurs de la cité céleste* and in several passages in my *Chronochromie*; there, birdsong is submitted to all kinds of manipulation in the manner of the composers of electronic music and *musique concrète*. It's a more dishonest attitude *vis-à-vis* nature but perhaps more honest in the work of a composer. I think that both attitudes are valid.

CLAUDE SAMUEL. When you choose the course of exactitude, do you want the listener to identify your bird landscapes precisely?

OLIVIER MESSIAEN. When one knows the bird and the landscape I want to depict, one should take a special pleasure in listening to the piece because one rediscovers these elements as one rediscovers friends, memories of childhood or certain things lost in a corner of memory; that, in any case, is what I feel. Nevertheless, the musical result is there and the listener who doesn't know birdsong may take pleasure in the music itself. Moreover, life reveals itself if the work is successful without identification being necessary. How many lovely portraits of past centuries whose original sitters we did not know nevertheless seem to us to be crying out with life and truth! We seem to recognise people we've never known because the pictures are successful.

CLAUDE SAMUEL. Yes, but looking at such portraits, we know that they concern a man taken for a model by the painter, whereas in the case of a listener who hears *La Rousserolle effarvatte*, do you think that the presence of birds compels recognition, particularly if the listener happens to be a city-dweller who sees pigeons in the streets but doesn't know what birdsong is?

OLIVIER MESSIAEN. That's his loss! He should go into the

country, and this would be good for his physical and moral welfare.

CLAUDE SAMUEL. But if he doesn't take this good advice, do you think that the "bird" idea would strike him?

OLIVIER MESSIAEN. If he knows birds in general, it must strike him. If he doesn't know them, he'll take pleasure in the music for itself, and, indeed, this might not be so bad.

CLAUDE SAMUEL. But the idea that listeners will take pleasure in the music itself without thinking of birds annoys you . . .

OLIVIER MESSIAEN. It would obviously be a pity, but identification is not an indispensable condition.

CLAUDE SAMUEL. Let's now consider birdsong from the angle of material. Are birds there, too, a source of riches?

OLIVIER MESSIAEN. Certainly! I spoke to you a moment ago of the song thrush with its incantatory repetitions: each strophe is built on very extraordinary rhythms, still richer than our Greek and Hindu rhythms.

CLAUDE SAMUEL. It leaves one wondering when one thinks of all the elaboration necessitated by the complexity of our own rhythms. Does this paradox seem normal to you?

OLIVIER MESSIAEN. I dare not reply . . . My answer would be that civilisation has spoilt us, has withdrawn our freshness of conception.

CLAUDE SAMUEL. In short, your task as a composer is to rediscover an element deeply enclosed in nature. Can you cite similar approaches, I mean of composers who have also used birdsong? Obviously one thinks of famous pieces like *The Goldfinch* by Vivaldi . . .

OLIVIER MESSIAEN. Or of the *Rossignol en amour* of Couperin, of the quotation of the cuckoo in Daquin and in the Pastoral Symphony of Beethoven . . . All of these bear very little resemblance to the actual birdsong, except the cuckoo because it's so easy to imitate! I even think that Couperin, given what he wrote, had never heard a nightingale, but this takes away nothing from the charm of the piece. It's sad, perhaps, but I think that I was the first composer to interest myself in birdsong. I'm not the first to have been interested in nature,

64

there were before me after all Berlioz and Wagner, who loved mountains, and Debussy, who was interested in wind, water, clouds, mists and all the most lovely and poetic phenomena; but evidently composers forgot birds. I am the first to have made scientific and, I hope, really accurate transcriptions of birdsong.

CLAUDE SAMUEL. This work is still a little disconcerting. When we spoke of rhythms, we noticed that your studies had served as a spring-board and coincided with contemporary discoveries, whereas I've the impression that your work as an ornithologist has had no echo from the young composers and places you in a position of disagreement with your time. In short, you are doing something completely exceptional.

OLIVIER MESSIAEN. Completely exceptional. I will even tell you that my pupils who know that I devote myself to this work are politely astounded. They dare not tell me that they find me crazy, but doubtless they think it; the most mischievous consider it a mania and compare me to those old maids who take their dogs out on a leash and caress kittens all day long, while those that are . . . I was going to say more perceptive, think that all the same I've discovered masters, a means of working and progressing, but they don't understand all the beauty and poetry, contenting themselves with being astonished . . .

CLAUDE SAMUEL. Because there is here, still, a mystery and we aren't really in the period of mysteries. I would add, but we've often repeated it, that you are—the man of mysteries?

Conversation 5

CLAUDE SAMUEL. If your output is considered today, a long curve of evolution may be easily discerned; and before tackling a systematic study of your works, it's advisable to determine the origin of this curve, that is to say the different influences that have contributed to the forging of your personality.

OLIVIER MESSIAEN. The greatest influence I received was from my mother, an influence all the more extraordinary in that it preceded my birth, because my mother, the poetess Cécile Sauvage, while awaiting me wrote a magnificent book of "prematernal" poetry called *L'Ame en bourgeon* (The soul in travail). This lyrical anticipation was followed by a fairytale education, mainly during the 1914 war, when my father and uncle were mobilised and when I found myself alone at Grenoble with my mother and grandmother; during all this period my mother brought me up in a climate of poetry and fairy-tales which, independently of my musical vocation, was at the origin of all that I did later. Indeed, such a climate enormously develops the imagination of a child and guides it towards intangible expressions which find their true end in music, the most intangible of all the arts.

CLAUDE SAMUEL. Who were the composers and what were the works which enabled you to penetrate the universe of music?

OLIVIER MESSIAEN. When I was a small boy, at Grenoble, between the ages of six and seven, I learnt the piano on my own and I even began to compose. Each year, like all children, I awaited the arrival of Christmas which brought me presents, but the presents which I listed in advance weren't toys, nor even pictures to be coloured or books: they were musical scores. I asked for, and received successively: Mozart's *Don Giovanni* and *Zauberflöte*, Gluck's *Alceste* and *Orphée*, *La Damnation de Faust* by Berlioz, Wagner's *Walküre* and *Siegfried*, over and above a few presents given me by friends of the family such as piano pieces by Debussy and Ravel, and in particular the *Estampes* and *Gaspard de la nuit*.

CLAUDE SAMUEL. The number of operas in this list surprises me all the more since, in your composing career, you've never shown the least predilection for this form.

OLIVIER MESSIAEN. It is strange. All day, I would declaim Shakespeare and, with the shrill voice of a small boy, I would sing all the roles in these operas, to the great despair of my family and of our neighbours.

CLAUDE SAMUEL. Can one discern, in your first compositions, the influence of the composers you've just mentioned?

OLIVIER MESSIAEN. Certainly I've always loved these composers and still do. I remember a day when, instead of playing with the other children, I went to sit on a stone seat in the big municipal garden at Grenoble, the old garden of the hôtel de Lesdisguières, which is near to the church of Saint-André, the law courts and the town hall. I'd just been bought excerpts from Gluck's *Orphée* and I was looking at the theme in F major in the big aria for Orphée in the first Act, which is probably the most beautiful phrase Gluck ever wrote, when I realised that I was "hearing" it. So, I could already "hear" a score—and I had only been doing music for a few months.

CLAUDE SAMUEL. Did you discover, in your youth, some composers who were then considered "modern"? You've mentioned Debussy ...

OLIVIER MESSIAEN. I mentioned Debussy's *Estampes*, which I knew when I left Grenoble, and Ravel's *Gaspard de la nuit*; I was quite ready for impressionist music which didn't even seem "modern" to me. Then I left for Nantes when my father, after the war, was appointed teacher of English there. During a stay of only six months in that city, I met several teachers who took a liking to me and gave me free lessons: the Misses Véron and

Gontran Arcouët for piano, and Jehan de Gibon for harmony. This last teacher, who was both poor and a very great artist, never forgot me. He wrote to me regularly throughout his life and I even had the great joy of seeing him again a few months before his death in the little town of Redon where he had gone to end his days. He made me work, as he should, at the textbook of Reber and Dubois, but he also gave me, when I was ten, a score of *Pelléas et Mélisande*. This was something quite different from the *Estampes*! It was a real bomb for a provincial teacher to put into the hands of quite a small boy.

This score was for me a revelation, love at first sight; I sang it, played and re-sang it time and time again. I recognise there probably the most decisive influence I have been subject to. And that, too, is an opera, isn't it?

CLAUDE SAMUEL. Let's speak now of your first published work.

OLIVIER MESSIAEN. They were the piano *Préludes* written in 1929.

CLAUDE SAMUEL. And these *Préludes*, as the title suggests, are in essence Debussyesque . . .

OLIVIER MESSIAEN. So they say, but it isn't absolutely true. I recognise that the sub-titles are quite Debussy-like: *"Les sons impalpables du rêve . . ."*, *"Un reflet dans le vent . . ."*.

But the music differs from that of Debussy by its use of my "modes of limited transposition" which are already very marked and even combined. They include polymodal passages, which are rather "peppered" for the time, and a few exercises in form; there may be found in these *Préludes* a sonata-form, an A-B-A form in which all the phrases are ternary, and a prelude built like those of Bach's fugues. Debussy never used form like this. Because of the modes used and perhaps also by reason of my being a pupil of Paul Dukas (the composer of *Ariane et Barbe-bleue* and of a "jewel scene", where each torrent of precious stones has a colour wedded to a tonality), the *Préludes* present a kind of sound-colour relationship. Finally, as regards rhythm, I was very far from Debussy's divine freedom.

CLAUDE SAMUEL. How do you regard this work, which you composed in your twentieth year, today?

OLIVIER MESSIAEN. With affection and even tenderness. There are some pretty harmonies which I wouldn't disown—and I've always liked the fifth and sixth préludes: *Les sons impalpables du rêve . . .*, and *Cloches d'angoisse et larmes d'adieu.*

CLAUDE SAMUEL. You've mentioned the name of Paul Dukas; who are the other teachers who influenced you?

OLIVIER MESSIAEN. I can name in order all the teachers I had at the Conservatoire. On my arrival in Paris, I first studied the piano with Georges Falkenberg, then harmony with Jean Gallon, and counterpoint and practically all musical theory in private lessons with Noël Gallon for about ten years. I won my fugue prize when I was with Georges Caussade, my accompaniment prize with Estyle, and my organ prize with Marcel Dupré who initiated me into plainsong, registration, improvisation and taught me organ technique. Finally, I worked at the timpani and percussion with Baggers (the only percussion teacher at that time), history of music and Greek rhythms with Maurice Emmanuel, composition and orchestration with Paul Dukas, who was my main teacher.

CLAUDE SAMUEL. During your apprenticeship at the Conservatoire, did you know the "modern" composers like Bartók or the "Viennese"?

OLIVIER MESSIAEN. At the time when I was in the composition class, those you call the "Viennese" were totally unknown in France, except Schoenberg. But, rightly, you're going to acknowledge my curiosity in this: I was the only student at the Conservatoire who had acquired Schoenberg's *Pierrot lunaire* and Stravinsky's *Rite of Spring*; moreover, I knew and liked all Stravinsky's other works.

CLAUDE SAMUEL. But was your sensibility nearer to *Pelléas, The Rite,* or *Pierrot?*

OLIVIER MESSIAEN. I was nearest to Debussy. I remained true to my childhood loves: Debussy, Mozart and Berlioz.

CLAUDE SAMUEL. And you only discovered Webern much later?

OLIVIER MESSIAEN. Yes, for the name of Webern had never been uttered at that time. Bartók was very well known and the big works of Stravinsky, but, in the way of future dodecaphony,

70

there was absolutely nothing but *Pierrot lunaire*. Berg had never been played in France, and all that was known about Webern was, I think, an article which he'd written in the *Revue Musicale* on serial procedure.

CLAUDE SAMUEL. Do you remember when you first heard a work of Webern's?

OLIVIER MESSIAEN. Much later, after the war.

CLAUDE SAMUEL. That's to say, after Webern's death?

OLIVIER MESSIAEN. Yes, nor did I know Berg's *Wozzeck* until then. On the other hand, I knew the *Lyric Suite* from my thirtieth year. I even had a score of it in my kitbag during my captivity.

CLAUDE SAMUEL. And when you finished your studies, about 1930, where did you stand in relation to the French composers of the preceding generation, I mean the composers of *"Les Six"*?

OLIVIER MESSIAEN. I can sum up my position in a word: nowhere. Moreover, I continued in that position. I was on the side: I greatly admired Honegger and Milhaud (and I still admire such masterpieces as Honegger's *Antigone* and Milhaud's *L'Homme et son Désir* and *La Création du Monde*), but I didn't approve at all of the movement directed by Cocteau—I don't speak of Cocteau the poet or film director, but of the Cocteau of *Coq et Harlequin*, torchbearer in a kind of musical renewal; no, I didn't approve at all of all this so-called simplification which took off from Gounod to drown in the "returns to Bach" and other similar things. I never agreed with this.

CLAUDE SAMUEL. And what of a composer like Erik Satie who also had his hour of glory at this time?

OLIVIER MESSIAEN. I found his music completely useless and devoid of interest.

CLAUDE SAMUEL. And your opinion hasn't changed?

OLIVIER MESSIAEN. No, no!

CLAUDE SAMUEL. There then is the starting point of your aesthetic position, and since this starting point exists in the concrete form of your piano *Préludes*, perhaps we might

71

now consider the whole of your output for piano. At what period did you think of renewing piano-writing?

OLIVIER MESSIAEN. As you know I've written a lot for piano, and not only for piano solo: the piano is present in the majority of my works. But there's obviously an enormous distance between the *Préludes* of 1929 and the *Visions de l'Amen* or the *Vingt Regards sur l'Enfant Jésus* which date from 1943 and 1944. And the *Catalogue d'Oiseaux*, which I composed in 1956 to 1958, marks a gigantic step from the works of 1944.

CLAUDE SAMUEL. Let's try to determine the constants of your pianistic language. They are due first of all to the fact that you yourself are a pianist . . .

OLIVIER MESSIAEN. Yes, I'm a pianist, but I never studied the piano very assiduously, and, moreover, I didn't get a piano prize át the Conservatoire; I worked at the piano partly on my own, and since, by a combination of circumstances, I entered the organ class, where I won a prize, I was above all a good organist before I turned to plainsong and improvisation. On the other hand, in the field of piano playing, it's obvious that I'll never have the transcendental virtuosity and the absolutely amazing technical possibilities of Yvonne Loriod. But I'm nevertheless a "good pianist"; in any case I have great facility in sight-reading, and my pupils will tell you this for, in my class, I sight-read anything and everything without making too many mistakes. I would add, and this perhaps is what characterises me, that I play the piano as if I were conducting an orchestra, that's to say turning the piano into a mock orchestra with a great range of timbres and accents. For me, this is a natural reaction, doubtless because I played many orchestral transcriptions when I was a child, notably the famous operas of which we spoke just now and which have certainly influenced my way of playing the piano.

CLAUDE SAMUEL. A moment ago you called to mind the "amazing possibilities" of Yvonne Loriod. To what extent have you thought of her exceptional knowledge of music and of her exceptional digital facility when you have written the works which she has, indeed, created?

OLIVIER MESSIAEN. It's óbvious that in writing the *Vingt Regards* or the *Catalogue d'Oiseaux*, I knew that they would be played by Yvonne Loriod; I could thus allow myself the greatest eccentricities, because everything is possible to her. I knew that I could imagine things that were very difficult, very extraordinary and very new, and that they would be played and played well.

CLAUDE SAMUEL. What are the elements that have contributed to the formation of your pianistic language?

OLIVIER MESSIAEN. I should perhaps tell you first what I like in piano music. I like Rameau very much and his harpsichord pieces, for the harpsichord is the ancestor of the piano. I also like Domenico Scarlatti for the same reason. Then, I adore Chopin, the *Ballades* as well as the *Préludes* and the *Etudes*, the *Scherzos* as well as the *Barcarolle*, the *Berceuse* and the 'Funeral March' Sonata: I love all Chopin, who is, to my mind, the greatest piano composer. He invented the most extraordinary passage-work, fingering and combinations.

Love of Chopin

CLAUDE SAMUEL. Is this a pianist's or composer's love?

OLIVIER MESSIAEN. I love Chopin *qua* pianist-composer and also *qua* colourist, for, in my view, he's a very great colourist. Because he only wrote for the piano, why should he be put in a little box?

Obviously, I love Debussy: I've always loved him. I also love the writing in some pages of Ravel (I think of *Gaspard de la nuit*, which is certainly a masterpiece). I would mention finally a work which has played a great part in my knowledge of the piano: Albeniz's *Ibéria*, which I discovered at about nineteen! I've often played and replayed the twelve pieces contained in its four books (above all *Almeira, El Polo* and *Lavapies*)... without attaining perfection, for they're of terrifying difficulty: I'll never be able to play them like Yvonne Loriod...

CLAUDE SAMUEL. ...who has recorded them. So there are the big piano cycles which have left their mark on you...

OLIVIER MESSIAEN. After that I see no "good piano music". There are perhaps some very beautiful pages, but they have no particular pianistic interest.

73

CLAUDE SAMUEL. You're thinking of Bartók and Prokofiev?

OLIVIER MESSIAEN. Yes; there are lucky finds in detail, two or three interesting innovations in Bartók's *Outdoor Suite*, and also the use of the slanted thumb in some of Prokofiev's passage-work. I'm afraid, however, that after Chopin we have to wait for Boulez to witness a transformation of the piano. Boulez's piano-writing uses brusque leaps with clawings and underhand attacks which are of an absolutely electrifying dynamism. This totally transforms the sonority of the piano in a way which had not been done previously.

CLAUDE SAMUEL. After having spoken of "the others", would you define the main lines of your piano output?

OLIVIER MESSIAEN. It's characterised, first of all, by the use of chords in clusters, which derive perhaps from the experience of organ mixtures. You know that mixtures are stops comprising several pipes per note, giving each note not only the pitch played but its harmonics, the octave, quint and tierce, etc ... The drawback with these artificial harmonics, which proceed in cascades with the note played, is their symmetry, since, perforce, one always gets the same resonances, the same octaves, the same quints and the same tierces. In my piano-writing, the chord-clusters would bring about the same result, but the chords are all different; so there is no symmetry and I've avoided an uninterrupted succession of quints and tierces which would have produced ridiculous parallelisms of fourths and sixths or of perfect chords. These chord-clusters give my writing an aspect of precious stones, a shimmer, a stained-glass quality which is rather characteristic.

In the second place, I will mention the innovations in the order of passage-work and fingering. Thus, in my *Vingt Regards*, I've used passages in contrary motion, the two hands violently spreading chords against each other with tiny clashes; this is a very rare procedure, used by harpists in *forte*, but still more powerful on the piano.

Another effect consists of laying the hand flat in attacking the four fingers with the thumb bedded as pivot; the hand is turned around the thumb and the four fingers are now to the right and now to the left of the thumb; this gives a "rebounding" technique which can be very brilliant. You'll find an example of this fingering towards the end of the *Regard de l'Esprit de Joie*.

I think I am one of the first to have used simultaneously the extreme treble and the extreme bass registers of the keyboard, not only for gentle effects but for those of power and of contrast. I've even combined *accelerando* and *rallentando* in my *Vingt Regards*; it's an extremely rare effect and hardly exists except in Bali; it may be found in the *Regard de l'Onction Terrible*.

Finally, in my *Catalogue d'Oiseaux*, a still greater number of innovations may be noted, because reproducing the timbre of birdsong has compelled me to constant inventions of chords, sonorities and combinations of sonorities and complexes of sounds which result in a piano which does not sound "harmonically" like other pianos. One example among a thousand is the timbre of the Blue Rock Thrush, rendered by a triple means: (a) the song is played in double-notes in a pentatonic mode by the right hand, (b) above the song, the left-hand crossing over gives a chromatic and slightly less loud version of the same line, (c) to render the echo of the song from the rocks where the bird sings (in the cliffs which overhang the blue sea at Cap l'Abeille and Cap Rederis near to Banyuls), complexes of sound in double arpeggios create a sonorous halo beneath the song, like the resonance of a bell—the ensemble of these three procedures gives a luminous, iridescent timbre haloed in blue.

CLAUDE SAMUEL.   You've mainly used the piano on its own, but you've also written the *Visions de l'Amen* for two pianos, and you've even associated the piano with the violin, clarinet and cello in your *Quatuor pour la fin du temps*. Indeed, the piano often plays an essential role in your orchestral works although you've never composed a classical piano concerto . . .

OLIVIER MESSIAEN.   Quite so, I've written no concertos; in my *Trois Petites Liturgies*, for example, the piano "material" is as important as the choir, vibraphone, ondes or strings.

CLAUDE SAMUEL.   Not more important?

OLIVIER MESSIAEN.   Yes; it's treated as an important soloist, but given the role of studding the texture with diamonds, which does not correspond to its role in a classical concerto.

CLAUDE SAMUEL. Why haven't you composed a "real" piano concerto?

OLIVIER MESSIAEN. Because I don't believe in concerto-form; most of the time it's extremely boring and, personally, in the form of masterpieces, I only know the twenty-two concertos by Mozart. All the others seem to me to be failures, excepting two or three very beautiful passages in the Concerto by Schumann, and a few moments in Franck's *Variations symphoniques* or in the concertos of Prokofiev.

CLAUDE SAMUEL. Isn't this attack on the piano concerto in fact against formal classical schemes? For you've displayed no more special affection in regard to the traditional sonata or symphony . . .

OLIVIER MESSIAEN. Like all my contemporaries.

CLAUDE SAMUEL. Let's say, some of your contemporaries. But why?

OLIVIER MESSIAEN. I consider that these forms are "finished". Just as one can no longer write a Mozartian opera with arias and recitatives, it's impossible to write, like Beethoven, a symphonic first movement with a theme which enters saying: 'I am the theme", and which after the development returns affirming: "It's still I, I'm the theme, do you recognise me?"

CLAUDE SAMUEL. As you've made a clear sweep of classical forms, on what formal frames do you rely?

OLIVIER MESSIAEN. I've not abandoned the eternal principle of development because this is inconceivable, nor that of variation which is also everlasting. I've used forms which, if not classical in an eighteenth-century sense, were nevertheless so in a distant past like the Greek triad: strophe, antistrophe, epode. For example, *The Alpine Chough*, at the beginning of my *Catalogue d'Oiseaux*, includes strophe, antistrophe and epode with two couplets, inserted between antistrophe and epode; so it is a blend of the couplet-refrain form with that of the triad. In *Chronochromie*, there are also two strophes, two antistrophes and one epode, which are framed by an introduction and a coda.

76

But it's in the *Catalogue d'Oiseaux* that you'll recognise my big formal innovation. There, instead of referring to an antique or classical mould or even to some mould I might have invented, I've sought to reproduce in condensed form the vivid march of the hours of day and night.

CLAUDE SAMUEL. That's the case of *The Reed Warbler* ...

OLIVIER MESSIAEN. ... and of most of the pieces of this collection. I'm preparing, moreover, a second collection which will be constituted in the same manner, based on my observations of nature.

CLAUDE SAMUEL. After this foray into formal problems which we'll return to later, could we take up again our consideration of your output? From the piano to the organ is only a step; but between your early and latest works for organ there lies an abyss ...

OLIVIER MESSIAEN. Without doubt. There's an enormous difference.

CLAUDE SAMUEL. Greater than in your pianistic production?

OLIVIER MESSIAEN. Certainly, because I held myself back in my early organ works, knowing that they would be played in church; then, when I began as organist at the Trinité, I was exposed to malevolence and the protests of parishioners, above all of the old ladies who heard the devil in the organ pipes.

CLAUDE SAMUEL. At this period, what did you offer your elderly lady parishioners?

OLIVIER MESSIAEN. My first published organ work, *Le Banquet céleste*: a very charming, tender, sweet and spring-like piece, which has nothing extraordinary about it! ... My second organ work doesn't deserve this title, because it's really a transcription with a few additions of an orchestral work: *L'Ascension*. Then came *L'Apparition de l'Eglise éternelle*, an enormous crescendo and descrescendo using all the power of the organ. It's quite a successful piece although very simple in its monolithic effect and its crushing use of the tutti, but one can't speak here of a renewal of organ-writing. This renewal began with *La Nativité du Seigneur*, a work which gained great success in France and abroad (without deserving it, for I've done much better). But *La*

Nativité with its Hindu rhythms nevertheless constituted a great change in organ music at a time when Franck represented the summit of modernism.

I arrive at my three best organ works: *Les Corps Glorieux* of 1939, the *Messe de la Pentecôte* of 1950, and the *Livre d'Orgue* of 1951. I think I've already told you that the *Messe de la Pentecôte* is the result of more than twenty years improvising; and moreover, after writing this piece, I've never improvised. As for my *Livre d'Orgue*, it's important for its rhythmic researches and conception of durations. In the last piece of the *Livre d'Orgue: Soixante-quatre durées*, I've tried to make the listener grasp some extremely long note-values, the differences between which are exceedingly small. It's very difficult for a human being to appreciate these. We are average-sized creatures of medium height and, alas, of average thinking; we're half-way between the microcosm and the macrocosm. So we perceive very long note-values with difficulty and the very tiny durations which could be the differences between these long durations with even greater difficulty. Take, for example, a note-value of sixty-three demisemiquavers, and a note-value of sixty-four demi-semiquavers: both are very long and the difference between them is almost imperceptible. It's a very perilous enterprise to put in the same pieces durations and differences of that order. It's still more perilous to treat these note-values as a scale of durations with regular permutations, going from the extremes to the centre, then combining them in retrograde canon, and to make their divisions audible by little counterpoints with shorter values. I don't know if I succeeded, but in any case, it's a little *tour de force*.

CLAUDE SAMUEL. Do you think that, after the fashion of *The Art of Fugue*, your *Livre d'Orgue* presents in the first place a theoretical interest?

OLIVIER MESSIAEN. Yes, in one sense. But there are also violent colours and new effects in it. Thus, *Les mains de l'Abîme* was written contemplating the meanderings of the torrent of the Romanche in the terrifying aspect of the gorges of the Infernet: this is a truly impressive abyss; I wanted to pay homage at the

78

same time to this vertigo and symbolically to the two gulfs of human misery and divine pity. As a motto, this verse by the Prophet Habakkuk: "The deep uttered his voice, and lifted up his hands on high". It concerns the depth of our misery, but another text in the Psalms says. "Deep calleth unto deep", that is to say, the deep of Man calls to the deep of God. According to the admirable commentary by Hello: "The abyss below must show death behind him, so that the abyss above shows life above him". To translate these vertiginous sentiments into music, I've juxtaposed the extremes of the organ, taking advantage of the wide range of the stops of the instrument; so I've given simultaneous sound to a very low voice which represents the bottom of the abyss of human misery, with a deep and terrifying sound, a little like the cavernous trumpetings and chants of Tibetan priests—you see we again return to magic—and, above, the voice of God replying. But it isn't a terrifying voice of thunder and lightning, it's a voice that is mysterious, distant, very high, almost tender and hardly audible. One has absolutely no idea of what one is hearing; one voice is so low, and the other so high, and the timbres are so strange that it's impossible to make out the notes. This strikes me as marvellously conveying the ideas of penitence, reverence and of vertigo before the Holy.

CLAUDE SAMUEL.   So, one of your works, where the experimental and didactic aspect is most obvious, is also a human and religious message. Isn't this bivalence one of the most noble characteristics of your music?

OLIVIER MESSIAEN.   That's true.

CLAUDE SAMUEL.   Let's speak more of your organ music. Do you think that it belongs to the tradition of the romantic organ?

OLIVIER MESSIAEN.   I've been reproached for it . . . for it is a reproach!

CLAUDE SAMUEL.   Why?

OLIVIER MESSIAEN.   I'm not ashamed of being a romantic. The romantics were magnificent craftsmen too often considered like cab-drivers who beat their breasts crying: "I am the Evil One!" A grotesque attitude! The romantics were aware of the beauties of nature, of the grandeur of divinity; they were grandiose, and

79

many of our contemporaries would gain from being "romantiscised".

So, I've no shame at being a romantic, but when it's said that my organ writing is romantic, it is a reproach—at least in the mouth of other organists. You know, indeed, the present tendency of organists to rediscover the organ of the eighteenth century: this tendency is expressed in the building of instruments of a clearer and brighter character, but also more refined and less powerful, with a great abundance of mixture stops. Present day builders have reason to restore to the organ its great originality, but they increasingly withdraw powerful reed stops and also rather rounded flue stops. This gives, I repeat, some very clear and bright instruments, perfect for contrapuntal music, for the work of Bach, Nicolas de Grigny and their contemporaries, but on which one can't play more powerful works, and this is after all a deficiency. I'm not hostile to this rather remarkable conception, but it should be possible to play everything on one instrument, and my love for the powerful, overwhelming organ (Berlioz called it "the pope of instruments") prevents me from preferring the classical type of instrument.

CLAUDE SAMUEL.   Your conception, then, is more romantic?

OLIVIER MESSIAEN.   I don't see why power should be condemned.

CLAUDE SAMUEL.   This isn't a reproach, but this power is primarily an attribute of the romantics.

OLIVIER MESSIAEN.   Perhaps. I'd also add that it's difficult to be powerful. One isn't powerful by wishing it: it's less easy to paint a large canvas than a small one.

CLAUDE SAMUEL.   Which, according to you, are the most outstanding personalities in the French Organ School of the twentieth century?

OLIVIER MESSIAEN.   I would cite the excellent composer Jehan Alain, who unhappily died before his time during the last war. I only met him once. Without really knowing each other, we followed near enough the same path, and it's possible that, if he'd lived longer, he would have gone in the same direction as myself.

CLAUDE SAMUEL. And if we go back further in this French School . . .

OLIVIER MESSIAEN. Well, in the School which preceded me, two names dominate all organ literature, those of Marcel Dupré and Charles Tournemire. In his time, my teacher Marcel Dupré was the greatest of all organ virtuosi, perhaps even the greatest of all the virtuosi who have ever existed; he was the Liszt of the organ. His music reflects this extraordinary virtuosity; he wrote pages of extreme difficulty and of great brilliance in toccata-style and he was the initiator of the ultra-staccato style, which obviously wasn't used by the classics. As for Charles Tournemire, he was an inspired man who is too little known; for a long time he was organist of Sainte-Clotilde, like César Franck, and he left a monument called *L'Orgue mystique*, comprising a complete office for all the Sundays and Feast Days with an *Introit, Offertoire, Elévation, Communion* and final "paraphrase".

CLAUDE SAMUEL. Let's jump a few decades to rediscover your work as organist, which was interrupted in 1951, the date of composition of your *Livre d'Orgue*. Has this interruption now come to an end?

OLIVIER MESSIAEN. Almost. Nevertheless, I have since written a little piece, commissioned from me for the *concours d'orgue* of the Conservatoire, called *Verset pour la fête de la Dédicace*.

CLAUDE SAMUEL. Will you forgive me if I consider this *Verset* as incidental to a composer who loves big cycles, and speak of an "interruption"? What's the cause of it?

OLIVIER MESSIAEN. The first reason is the lure of the orchestra and piano awoken in me, but there's also a basely material reason: for two years my instrument at the Trinité has been in course of restoration by order of the Paris municipality, and I must confess that I no longer play at all.*

CLAUDE SAMUEL. Yes, but this silence began in 1951 . . . Then I ask myself if, with your *Livre d'Orgue*, you hadn't arrived at a summit, at a point of achievement seemingly impossible to go beyond at the present time?

* In October, 1966, Olivier Messiaen, on completion of the restoration, once again took possession of the organ at the Trinité.

81

OLIVIER MESSIAEN. Perhaps . . .

CLAUDE SAMUEL. As to the future?

OLIVIER MESSIAEN. You must wait and see.

CLAUDE SAMUEL. Let's place a few points of suspension then and consider your output devoted to the human voice. These aren't the best-known works, but they're none the less revealing.

OLIVIER MESSIAEN. I've composed three big song cycles: the *Poèmes pour Mi*, the *Chants de terre et de ciel*, and *Harawi*. These three cycles are written for piano and voice, and only the first of them has been orchestrated; they're also characterised by the fact that I've called for a dramatic soprano voice on account of my admiration for Marcelle Bunlet, a marvellous singer and admirable musician who had a very flexible voice and a very extended tessitura, and who easily sang Isolde, Kundry and Brünnhilde. So I intended for her my song cycles which are very long, very tiring for the breath, and require a very wide vocal range. For all these reasons, it is understandable why few singers have tackled them and why these pieces, as you've noticed, are less known than others.

CLAUDE SAMUEL. How would you define your vocal writing?

OLIVIER MESSIAEN. I think that I write quite well for the voice because all that I've written for the voice I've sung myself. I've obviously a horrible composer's voice, but all the same I'm aware of what a theatrical scene is—remember my Shakespearean beginnings. I'm equally aware of the problems of diction, of the phonetic values of vowels and consonants, of the importance of breathing, of the good places to take breath, and the different registers of the voice.

CLAUDE SAMUEL. Since you profess such a love for the theatre and since you understand voices well, I repeat a question which I've already asked you: for what reason have you never written operas?

OLIVIER MESSIAEN. I've never written operas because I think that music drama is a formula, not false, but complex, which blends two genres; and you will agree with me that, in the course of musical history, opera came late and that at the present time it is practically dead.

Without doubt, opera gave rise to absolutely extraordinary works, such as Monteverdi's *Orfeo*, the opera-ballets of Rameau, Mozart's immortal masterpieces—*Don Giovanni*, *Die Zauberflöte*, and *Le nozze di Figaro*—Wagner's *Ring* cycle, operas with choruses of the type of *Boris Godunov*, and finally the two total but exceptional successes which are *Pelléas* and *Wozzeck*. Now, none of these formulae can be repeated: it's impossible in our day to rework the *Leitmotiv* or operas with alternating arias and recitatives; all this, if you'll excuse me, is out of date. What's to be done, then? A new formula must be found; some exist, however: for example, the Japanese *Noh* and the Balinese theatre. These are valid formulae, but imagine a French composer, even a well-known one, going to propose to an opera director in France something in the style of the Balinese theatre or Japanese *Noh* . . . he'd be told he was crazy, that the public wouldn't come, that it would cost too much, and that it would be better to give up the idea.

CLAUDE SAMUEL. Your position in regard to opera seems perfectly clear to me, and since we made this digression in considering the voice, we may add that you've also used *a cappella* choirs, notably in the *Cinq Rechants*.

OLIVIER MESSIAEN. I consider the *Cinq Rechants* one of my best works and am very fond of it. Similarly, I'm very much attached to *Harawi*, because these two works constitute a second and third "Tristan" beside *Turangalîla*; moreover, the *Cinq Rechants* represent an indirect tribute to the *Printemps* of Claude Le Jeune: indeed, they're in strophic form with couplets called *"chants"* and refrains called *"rechants"*, exactly like the *Printemps* of Claude Le Jeune. In this work, I've also made great use of Hindu rhythms (the deçî-tâlas of ancient India), and also of developed non-retrogradable rhythms. In the sixth of my *Vingt Regards*, I use a non-retrogradable rhythm which is developed by added values, then by contradictions to right and left, and you'll appreciate that since non-retrogradable rhythms are composed of two symmetrical retrograde groups, one on the right, the other on the left of a central value, it's necessary that there should be a symmetry between right and left for the added

83

and contracting values. On the other hand, when I develop the central values, I have no right to change those on the right and left, but only the central values may be augmented or diminished; this is what I've done in the three couplets of the third of my *Cinq Rechants*. Still in my *Cinq Rechants*, I would draw attention to another peculiarity, in a field where I've been preceded by Berlioz (as in the chorus of demons in *La Damnation de Faust*): the use of an "invented" language. I composed the *Cinq Rechants* on a poem written partly in French, but mainly in a new language sometimes resembling Sanskrit and sometimes Quechua (the old Peruvian language): it amounts really to words invented by reason of their phonetic qualities, words of which the vowels and consonants are arbitrarily chosen to correspond to certain rhythms and certain registers of the voice.

CLAUDE SAMUEL. Alongside the *Cinq Rechants* can be placed a work which unites choirs, the Ondes Martenot, a solo piano, a vibraphone and an instrumental ensemble: the *Trois Petites Liturgies de la Présence Divine*, these *Liturgies* which, on several counts, seem to occupy a decisive place in your output.

OLIVIER MESSIAEN. This is without doubt the most popular of my works, and this popularity seems to me explained by the presence of well-defined and very melodious themes. In any case, it's a work which won the greatest success right away ...

CLAUDE SAMUEL. ... even though its first performance instigated a scandal ...

OLIVIER MESSIAEN. No, it's success was immediate—at least with the public! It only caused a scandal in the minds of certain colleagues and in the articles of certain critics; some of them let themselves go to their hearts content, and emptied dustbins on my head for ten years after this work. But the public always went along with me and now the work is well beyond its hundredth performance.

CLAUDE SAMUEL. At the time of the first performance of the *Liturgies* in 1945, did the critical reaction disturb you?

OLIVIER MESSIAEN. It deeply amazed me, above all. I was astounded by this reaction, which I still can't understand today.

The work was obviously very daring in its musical aesthetic and in its combination of timbres, but it didn't justify such an outburst of fury. I imagine it was a kind of native mistrust by right-minded people, well ensconced in their armchairs with comfortable slippers, and opposed to everything out of the ordinary, especially in the spiritual domain—for this work is first of all a very great act of faith, and the poem is steeped with texts from the Holy Scriptures: the Gospels, Epistles, the Song of Songs, Psalms and the Book of Revelation, the most beautiful texts of Saint John and Saint Paul, and even passages from Saint Thomas and the "Imitation of Christ". Of course, the people attacking me didn't know these texts, they understood nothing of them—but they were all the same disturbed in their quietude! Excuse this comparison of inordinate pride: but this is how stones were once thrown at the prophets of Israel . . .

CLAUDE SAMUEL. You speak of the "popularity" of the *Petites Liturgies*. Yet I consider that in the matter of popularity the *Turangalîla-Symphonie* goes beyond the *Liturgies*.

OLIVIER MESSIAEN. It is indeed more popular, but not in the same sense. The subject is more accessible since it's a "Tristan and Isolde" and human love touches all men and women. *Turangalîla* also reaches the big crowds thanks to a considerable volume of orchestral sound.

CLAUDE SAMUEL. From the point of view of instrumental writing, do you think that the *Turangalîla-Symphonie* constitutes the best résumé of your aesthetic?

OLIVIER MESSIAEN. It's one of my works that is richest in discoveries; it's also the most melodious, the warmest, the most dynamic and the most coloured.

CLAUDE SAMUEL. In relation to *Turangalîla*, how do you consider your later orchestral scores?

OLIVIER MESSIAEN. There's a fundamental difference: the later works contain much more birdsong, and this makes a strong contribution to the renewal of my aesthetic.

CLAUDE SAMUEL. One thinks of *Le Réveil des Oiseaux* and of *Oiseaux exotiques*.

OLIVIER MESSIAEN. *Le Réveil des Oiseaux* and *Oiseaux exotiques* are two very special works and, in a sense, unique in my output: they contain *only* birdsong!

Actually, in *Oiseaux exotiques*, I've associated percussion with the woodwind, brass, xylophone and piano, and this percussion obviously plays no part in birdsong, it constitutes a strophic support based on rhythms, verses, metres and Greek measures and also on Hindu rhythms, all juxtaposed: the strophic form (with diminutions effected on Karnatic rhythms and Indian deçî-tâlas), evolves independently of the birdsong with its much greater freedom. So there's a blend of strictness and freedom, and, all the same, a certain part of composition in the birdsong material used, since without permission I've placed side by side the birds of China, India, Malaya, and of the North and South Americas, that is to say, birds that never meet. In *Le Réveil des Oiseaux* the presentation is much more accurate: there's only birdsong, without any added rhythm or counterpoint, and the singing birds may be found really united in nature; it's a completely truthful work. It concerns an awakening of birds at the beginning of a spring morning; the cycle goes from midnight to noon: night songs, awakening at four in the morning, a big tutti of birds stopped by the sunrise, midday songs—the great silence of noon.

CLAUDE SAMUEL. And *Chronochromie*?

OLIVIER MESSIAEN. *Chronochromie* is the type of polyvalent or, at least, bivalent work of which you were speaking a moment ago: a work where sometimes technical effort prevails over natural material, and sometimes the natural material takes first place. In the formal sphere, *Chronochromie* divides into seven compulsorily linked sections: introduction, strophe, antistrophe, a second strophe, and a second antistrophe, an epode completely different from all the rest, then coda. In all, it's a Greek triad with a doubling of the strophe and antistrophe, the epode being separate, and the whole framed by the introduction and coda. The introduction and coda use the same musical material arranged in a very different manner with other notes and other instrumentation. The two strophes and two antistrophes also have the same material each in relation to the other, but this material is used very differently, with other counterpoints, other rhythms, other chord-colours and timbres. Finally, the epode stands alone.

CLAUDE SAMUEL. A certain passage of *Chronochromie* where the strings are extremely divided generally causes the public to shiver . . .

OLIVIER MESSIAEN. Yes, let's frankly admit that this passage does cause a scandal. It's written for eighteen solo strings, twelve violins, four violas and two cellos—and it's made up of eighteen birdsongs, French birds which sing together and the names of which I'll give you, in order of entry on the scene: four Blackbirds, a Yellowhammer, a Goldfinch, a Chiffchaff, a Whitethroat, a Lesser Whitethroat, two Chaffinches, a Nightingale, a fifth and sixth Thrush, a Greenfinch, two Golden Orioles of which one is the echo of the other, and a little further away, a Linnet. These birdsongs enter one after another rather as in a fugue, the entries proceeding in a descending scale, then all the voices go forward imperturbably above each other, making up a counterpoint of eighteen real parts totally independent of each other for at least ten minutes.

CLAUDE SAMUEL. Ornithologist that you are, can eighteen birdsongs simultaneously producing such a music be observed in nature?

OLIVIER MESSIAEN. But of course! This exists in nature, above all at daybreak when one can often hear extremely complicated counterpoints made by birds of very different types, united by a rather similar habitat, singing together.

CLAUDE SAMUEL. But why wouldn't a listener, taken into a wood while this birdsong is going on, be scandalised, if he is shocked by hearing your musical transcription?

OLIVIER MESSIAEN. If he was taken to the edge of a wood, or into a park, he would have at the same time the beauties of the light, the perfume of dew on the leaves, the perfumes of the flowers; he would have all the context of landscape, scents, colours and thermal sensations which he is used to and which make the aural phenomenon very natural—whereas I have obviously separated this extraordinary counterpoint from its context: that's what provokes a scandal. I would add that the individual who hears these birdsongs in nature gives them minimal attention, precisely because of their context; he perceives the colours, scents and sounds as a whole, and if he were asked to isolate them from each other, he'd be very embarrassed. When I find myself in this situation, I am equally sensitive to colours and perfumes, but I listen especially to the song because I have come to note it; my hearing is much more profound and far sharper than that of the simple pedestrian.

CLAUDE SAMUEL. Is this famous passage of great difficulty in execution?

OLIVIER MESSIAEN. It's fearfully difficult because no counterpoint or rhythm is alike, and there's no harmonic control: the lost instrumentalist can never correct himself for he hears around him a hubbub so confused that he can distinguish no guide mark; and if the conductor makes the least error, everyone is lost.

CLAUDE SAMUEL. You have pronounced the term "confused hubbub", which might be considered a pejorative judgment; but is this the aim you've sought for in this passage?

OLIVIER MESSIAEN. No, it isn't the aim, but it's the impression felt by the instrumentalist in the middle of the orchestra, that is to say in an unfavourable listening place, or also felt by an audience which, although well-placed in the hall, doesn't hear properly.

CLAUDE SAMUEL. What rules must be observed to "hear properly"?

OLIVIER MESSIAEN. First of all, to arrive at the concert with an open mind, without a hate for the composer; then to love nature, knowing how to appreciate it in all its manifestations, sounds as well as colours, colours as well as perfumes, and perhaps to harbour a thought of a musical nature allowing one to realise that in this apparent disorder, that in this lack of harmonic control, there are chordal colours hinted at, and that in this lack of rhythm, there are thousands of superimposed rhythms which combine in a great rhythm and in blocks of duration.

CLAUDE SAMUEL. You are in fact the grand director of these harmonies which meet at the will of birdsong.

OLIVIER MESSIAEN. Absolutely.

CLAUDE SAMUEL. To understand music of such complexity, wouldn't it be better to associate listening with a reading of the score?

OLIVIER MESSIAEN. Your question is very imprudent, because there are without doubt few musicians capable of reading this passage, to read and hear it in the mind's ear; I myself am obliged to read it very slowly to let nothing escape. I am quite unable to hear it in my mind in tempo, and I defy anyone to do that; but it's obviously easier in an actual performance, though even then it demands great attention and concentration.

CLAUDE SAMUEL. In a general way, do you think it's profitable to combine direct hearing with score-reading?

OLIVIER MESSIAEN. It's indispensable for the composer who wishes to learn how to orchestrate like this.

CLAUDE SAMUEL. But for the average listener?

OLIVIER MESSIAEN. For the average listener, it's a supplementary pleasure, because over and above the emotion felt at the beauty of the music and its timbres, he'll grasp the construction of the work better; but, for the majority of listeners, this score-reading is impossible and would even be detrimental, since, not knowing how to read a score, they would get lost, and instead of listening correctly, would spend their time turning the pages vacantly.

CLAUDE SAMUEL. Before leaving the aviary of *Chronochromie*, would you explain the precise meaning of the work's title?

OLIVIER MESSIAEN. This title unites two Greek words: *khronos*, which means time, and *khroma*, which means colour. As in composite words the terms are generally inverted, time precedes colour here. In fact *Chronochromie* means "Colour of Time".

The most important parts of *Chronochromie*, that is to say the "strophes", are based on symmetrical permutations. I won't give you an explanation in numbers of these permutations, which would be very complicated, necessitating drawings and heaps of numbers—I've made a table of these permutations which will appear in my *Traité de Rythme* which runs to one hundred and fifty pages; but a little demonstration is necessary all the same. Here it is:

You know that the number of permutations of several distinct objects rises enormously with each addition of a new unit to the chosen objects. Thus, three objects have six possible permutations, seven objects have 5,040 possible permutations, while twelve objects have 479,001,600 possible permutations. Let's choose a chromatic scale of durations going from a demi-semiquaver to a semibreve, thus from one to thirty-two demisemiquavers, with all the intermediate note-values. If I wanted to seek out and use the permutations, there are so many that I would need half a lifetime to write them out and several years to play them. One must choose, therefore, and choose with the maximum chance of dissimilarity between one permutation and another. To arrive at this, I read my scale of chromatic values in a certain order, then, having written down the result, I number from 1 to 32 the succession of note-values obtained, then I read my result thus numbered in the *same order* as the first time; I write down this second result and again number from 1 to 32 the succession of numbers obtained. Then I read my second result in the same order as the first time, which gives yet a third result, then I read my third result in the same order as the first time: I do the same thing for the fourth result, and so on until I arrive again at the chromatic scale of durations with which I began. This gives a reasonable number of permutations (not too far from the number of objects chosen), and also permutations sufficiently different to be juxtaposed and superimposed.

In the two "strophes" of *Chronochromie* there are three superimposed unfoldings of three lines of permutations of the 32 note-values: superimposition of the permutations 1, 2, and 3, in the first strophe—superimposition of the permutations 22, 23, 24 in the second strophe. So that the listener may hear the unfolding of these permutations I've coloured my note-values in three ways: by "minting", by timbre, and by strains of chords.

First coloration: *the sub-division of note-values.* In a long unfolding of durations, in order to appreciate the tiny differences between the long durations, the sense of the unit of value (here, the demisemiquaver) must be preserved. The woodwind, glockenspiel and xylophone will "mint" the durations by various rapid counterpoints of birdsong containing many short values, among them the demisemiquaver (which will be constantly recalled to the memory).

Second coloration: *timbre.* Each unfolding of durations is entrusted to metallic percussion instruments, different in timbre, intensity and pitch. The upper unfolding is entrusted to three gongs, pianissimo—the central unfolding to a peal of bells, forte—the lower unfolding to a suspended cymbal, a Chinese cymbal and a tam-tam, pianissimo.

Third coloration: *strains of chords.* This is by far the most effective. The attacks of the metallic percussion are doubled, underlined and prolonged by chords on twenty-two solo strings—chords belonging to three kinds of harmonic coloration. The line of gongs goes with seven violins which play "chords on the dominant", changing continually in position and transposition. The line of the suspended cymbal, Chinese cymbal and tam-tam goes with three violas and four cellos which play "chords of contracting resonance". One note-value will be linked to a red sonority flecked with blue—another will be linked to a milky white sonorous complex embellished with orange and hemmed with gold—another will use green, orange and violet in parallel bands—another will be pale grey with green and violet reflections—another will be frankly violet or frankly red. Juxtaposed or superimposed, all will be made prominent by colorations, colour serving to reveal the cut in Time.

It is the two strophes of *Chronochromie* which decided the title of the work. Durations and permutations of durations made perceptible by sonorous colorations (the ones explaining the others): this is truly a "Colour of Time", a *"Chronochromie".*

In the *Sept Haïkaï* rhythmic researches may also be found, but the procedure is not at all the same, as the title hints. The *Sept Haïkaï* result from the stunning impression made by Japan when I made a concert tour there with Yvonne Loriod. Between the various concerts, my impresario, Madame Fumi Yamaguchi, had very astutely prepared some resting resorts which would allow us to make contact with Japanese music, composers and birds. So I was able to hear in Karuizawa, Subashiri and, in woodland, by Lake Yamanaka, a large number of Japanese birds: I was accompanied by a Japanese ornithologist (with whom, as I speak neither Japanese nor English, I conversed in Latin, since fortunately birds, like trees and flowers, have Latin names).

So I composed the *Sept Haïkaï* at the conclusion of my journey to Japan, and I must stress their instrumental composition: the work is written for eleven woodwind—a piccolo, a flute, two oboes, a cor anglais, an E flat clarinet, two clarinets, a bass-clarinet and two bassoons, and two brass instruments, a trumpet and a trombone, and all these instruments are intended to represent birdsong. The woodwind play chords to underline the timbres of the different Japanese birds and the brass reinforce the ringing character of some of these birds' song, notably the *Uguisu* (the Japanese Warbler) and the *Hototoguisu* (the Little Grey-headed Cuckoo). Furthermore, there are two keyboard soloists, a xylophone and a marimba, that play passages in birdsong of great virtuosity—particularly those of the *Kibitaki* (Narcissus Flycatcher) and of the *San kô chô* (Paradise Flycatcher). Finally, a solo piano is entrusted with big cadenzas. Without having composed real concertos, I have nevertheless written numerous piano cadenzas in my orchestral works; there are five in the *Haïkaï*, they're very brilliant and contain both birdsong and passagework calculated to show off the instrument. Finally, the *Haïkaï* include some percussion: a set of cencerros, a set of crotales, a triangle, eighteen tubular bells, two small Turkish cymbals, two gongs, a Chinese cymbal and two tam-tams. You will note that all these instruments are of metallic character and are variations of a bell (which is perhaps the percussion

92

instrument I prefer).

But that isn't all: there are eight violins which are treated with total contempt. They're only there to produce grating sounds imitating the *Shô* or mouth organ, for this work associates with Japanese birds the landscape and traditional music of Japan. The central piece is entitled *Gagaku*, from the name of seventh century Japanese music, a noble form of music played at the Court of the Emperor, which was always played there and is still played there today, as I was able to observe. This music uses mainly the timbre of the *Shô* (which I've replaced by the eight violins), and of the *Hichirki*, a little, primitive and extremely shrill oboe (which I've replaced by a trumpet always doubled by a cor anglais). The ensemble established grating chords above the melody, "as the sky", say the Japanese, "is above the earth", in privileged, contradictory and unexpected places.

The fifth piece is entitled *Miyajima et le Torii dans la mer*. It evokes the most beautiful landscape in Japan: a gently mountainous island with a hill covered with *matsu* (a very green Japanese pine the decorative branches of which are gnarled like the arms of an old witch); at the foot of this island stands a magnificent Shinto temple, white, red and gold facing the blue sea—and what a blue!—and plunging its feet in the sea, before the temple, and opening on to the invisible, that is to say on to the true temple, there's a *Torii* (a porch extremely simple in form and coloured red). You can imagine all these mingled colours, the green of the Japanese pines, the white and gold of the Shinto temple, the blue of the sea, and the red of the *Torii* . . . That's what I've wanted to translate almost literally into my music. The piece is really green, red, gold and blue, and I've even added some other colours—violet, lilac, violet purple (my favourite colours)—by combining different sounds and different instrumental timbres.

Finally, two pieces are entirely dedicated to Birds: *Yamanaka-Cadenza* in which are assembled the birds I heard in woodland, by Lake Yamanaka, and *Les oiseaux de Karuizawa*. Karuizawa is a magnificent site, past the rice-fields on the outskirts of Tokyo, in the midst of extremely tortuous and dented mountains overhung by a still active volcano, Asama. Karuizawa, where I spent several days noting birdsong, is full of torrents, little gorges and forests of *matsu* and azaleas, those marvellous flowers of delicate and refined shape and of a ravishing pink or red colour! There are thousands of them, millions of azaleas, growing quite naturally in thickets without need of any cultivation. Obviously, all this attracts thousands of birds and it can be said that almost all the species of Japanese birds may be found together in this district of Karuizawa.

CLAUDE SAMUEL. So much then for the birds and colours mingled in the *Sept Haïkaï*. You then forgot Japan to unite your various preoccupations in a well-balanced manner within a new work: *Couleurs de la Cité céleste*.

OLIVIER MESSIAEN. The *Couleurs de la Cité céleste* was born of a strange commission; Dr Heinrich Strobel had asked me to write a work for three trombones and three xylophones. I'd accepted but was very unhappy, for I couldn't see how to use these instruments. After long reflection, I finally thought that the trombones had an apocalyptic sound, so I re-read the Book of Revelation and looked for quotations from it. Then I was struck by the percussive sound of the three xylophones, which allowed me to use birdsong provided that I could add a piano; still thinking of the birds, I thought it perhaps necessary to have a few clarinets to vary the timbres and, reviewing all these ideas, I added to the three trombones a little trumpet in D, three trumpets and two horns in F, as well as a bass trombone; I changed the three xylophones to one xylophone, one xylorimba and a marimba; I added the piano solo, the three clarinets and finally the metallic percussion: a set of cencerros, a set of bells, four gongs and two tam-tams.

As you've noticed, this work sums up all my preoccupations. First of all my religious preoccupations, since it has its source in five quotations from Revelation. Then my love of the mysterious, of magic, of enchantment, for these quotations from Revelation are extraordinary, extravagant, surrealistic and terrifying. Look at this one: "and to the star was given the key of the bottomless pit."

This has allowed me to imagine such effects as the alliance of very low trombone pedal-notes to the shrill resonance of three clarinets and to the deep rolls of the tam-tam. To this is added the idea of *colour* which you already find in the title: these *Couleurs de la Cité céleste* are the colours of Celestial Jerusalem, that is to say Paradise. Now, Paradise is represented in the Book of Revelation as a shimmering of colours and here again we come across the stained glass which fired me to enthusiasm in my youth. You know that to the master artists in stained glass of the Middle Ages, a stained-glass window was in the first place a lesson by images; enclosed within the leaden trefoils, almond-shapes and stars could be recognised a quantity of tiny figures representing the life of Christ, the Blessed Virgin and the Saints and their corresponding Old Testament symbols: it was a Holy History and a Catechism. When the window is viewed at a distance, the figures are too small to distinguish, but one is dazzled by colours: for example, a window dominated by blues and reds (even with a few patches of yellow and green) produces in the eye a sensation of an enormous violet. It happens that Saint John, in his Book of Revelation, described his celestial visions in the same way: so, when he spoke of divinity he didn't name it but said: "and there was a rainbow round about the throne", the idea of majesty being associated with the idea of dazzling colour. When he spoke of the Holy City, he said: "and her light was like unto a stone most precious, even like a jasper stone, clear as crystal." You know that jasper is mottled with various colours; as for jasper crystal, it's an extremely rare stone which should not only sport all the colours of the rainbow but also be translucent. Finally, Saint John says, "And the foundations of the wall of the city were garnished with all manner of precious stones: ... jasper, sapphire, chalcedony, emerald, sardonyx, sardine, chrysolite, beryl, topaz, chrysoprase, jacinth and amethyst". (I'd ask you to note that the colours of these stones give us all the colours of the rainbow.)

So I've tried to express in my work the colours mentioned in Revelation, and I think I've never been so deep into the sound–colour relationship: certain sound combinations really correspond to certain colour combinations, and I've noted the names of these colours on the score in order to impress this vision on the conductor who will, in his turn, transmit this vision to the players he directs: the brass should, dare I say it, "play red", the woodwind should "play blue", etc...

Moreover, the *Couleurs de la Cité céleste* contain, like the *Sept Haïkaï* and the *Oiseaux exotiques,* Hindu and Greek rhythms, and, like *Chronochromie,* symmetrical permutations of durations. There are also to be found plainsong themes; I had used plainsong themes in the past, but only partially, in *La Nativité du Seigneur* and in one or two pieces of my *Vingt Regards,* then I had abandoned them, and I took this idea up again because plainsong conceals some marvellous melodies. I chose four alleluias: the alleluia for the Eighth Sunday after Whitsun, the alleluia for the Fourth Sunday after Easter, the alleluia for the Dedication, and the alleluia for the Holy Sacrament. Finally, I used birdsong both for its intrinsic beauty and as a symbol of heavenly joy, and as I had done before in my *Oiseaux exotiques,* I took birdsong borrowed from different countries, birdsong that would never be found together.

CLAUDE SAMUEL.   An imaginary museum...

OLIVIER MESSIAEN.   Yes, to take up Malraux's formula, it's an imaginary museum of birdsong: birds from New Zealand, the Argentine Republic, Brazil, Venezuela and Canada.

CLAUDE SAMUEL.   Evocations of journeys?

OLIVIER MESSIAEN.   I made a stay in the Argentine where I heard two very common birds: the Hornero, which is the symbol of the country, and the Benteveo, the name of which means "I saw you all right." A few years ago I was also in Canada where I heard the song of the Western Meadowlark *(Sturnella neglecta).* These three birds and also the New Zealand Tui and Bellbird, the Barred-wing Wren Babbler and Mocking-bird from Venezuela, the Arapanga and Greyish Saltator from Brazil and many others—all this I've used in the *Couleurs de la Cité céleste.*

CLAUDE SAMUEL.   You've told us that these *Couleurs de la Cité céleste* originated in a commission from Dr Heinrich Strobel. Your work as a composer actually responds to commissions as numerous as they are varied, but I'd like to dwell on one of the latest to date: a commission by the State which is the origin of *Et exspecto resurrectionem mortuorum*.

OLIVIER MESSIAEN. Which means "And I await the resurrection of the dead". This score was commissioned from me by Andre Malraux. The five sections of the work are based on texts from the Holy Scriptures dealing with the resurrection of the dead, with the resurrection of Christ (instrumental cause and pledge of our resurrection), and of the life of the Heavenly Bodies which follow the resurrection of the dead, the applause of the angels and the resonances of the stars which accompany the moment of resurrection.

I assigned this work to a rather exceptional ensemble. It brings together a woodwind ensemble comprising eighteen instruments, an ensemble of seventeen brass: a small trumpet in D, three trumpets, six horns, three trombones, a bass trombone, a tuba, a bass saxhorn in B flat (a military band instrument similar to the Wagner bass tubas), and percussion, those metallic percussion instruments of which I'm particularly fond.

CLAUDE SAMUEL. It should be added that you have some recognised percussionists in the Strasbourg group.

OLIVIER MESSIAEN. Yes, indeed, it's for them that I've written most of my latest works, because they're admirable and they play some instruments with marvellous resonances. This concerns the three sets of concerros, a set of tubular bells, six gongs and three tam-tams.

In my score will be found, above all, religious ideas corresponding to the quotations from Holy Scripture that I've assembled, but there will also be found, very symbolically, two birdsongs: that of the Uirapuru and that of the Short-toed Lark. The Uirapuru *(Leucolepsis modulator)* is a bird of the Amazon, which is heard, it is supposed, at the moment of death, and which symbolises here this interior voice which will be the voice of Christ drawing the dead to their sleep and giving the signal for imminent resurrection. The Short-toed Lark is a sensational and inspired singer that has disappeared from France because it's been much hunted and killed, but which still exists in

Greece and Spain; its song is extraordinary for its chirping alleluia-like virtuosity: here it symbolises heavenly joy and one of the four attributes of the Heavenly Bodies, the "gift of agility".

I would add that *Et exspecto resurrectionem mortuorum* was first performed on two ceremonial occasions, the first discreet, since André Malraux wanted the work to be played before a few initiates, without a big audience, in a kind of semi-private session and in a place very suited to my religious thought and to the colours which I love: in the midst of the most beautiful stained glass in Paris, in a place where the light is irradiated in blues, reds, golds and extraordinary violets. I refer to the Sainte-Chapelle, that marvellous church, completely glazed with stained glass, which was built to the order of Saint-Louis for the Crown of Thorns to be deposited in.

The second performance took place in the presence of General de Gaulle in Chartres Cathedral, a Marian sanctuary, another high place of Christianity, famous not only for its two towers, one Roman, the other Gothic, but also for its marvellous porches and its statuary as well as for its extraordinary stained glass and the famous blue of Chartres.

CLAUDE SAMUEL. One last word on the semi-private first performance at the Sainte-Chapelle: the privileged audience invited to this event were struck not only by the play of light but also by the absolutely unaccustomed acoustic. Do you think that this acoustic was able to give a new dimension to this score, or did you also imagine this while composing it?

OLIVIER MESSIAEN. I conceived it to be played in a church, taking resonance for granted, also the ambience and even the echoing of sounds that can be obtained in such a place. I even wanted it to be played in the open air and on a mountain height, on the Grave, facing the Glacier de la Meije, in those powerful and solemn landscapes that are my true homeland. There, by the play of sunlight on the whiteness of the ice, I would obtain visually the second symbol which circulates in my music, the principal attribute of the Heavenly Bodies, the Gift of Light . . .

CLAUDE SAMUEL. The evocation of *Et exspecto resurrectionem mortuorum* leads us to the present time. Have you some projects you could confide to me?

OLIVIER MESSIAEN.   A project prematurely revealed is spoilt. A Chinese proverb says: "The future is as dark as lacquer."

CLAUDE SAMUEL.   Let's not worry about Chinese proverbs, although everything leads me to suppose that a new work is imminent. . . .

OLIVIER MESSIAEN.   Yes, of course, I'm always thinking of the work I'm going to compose during the summer, which is my big period of work.

CLAUDE SAMUEL.   Do you live with the works you're about to write for a long time before actually writing them?

OLIVIER MESSIAEN.   I think so, but often in an unconfessed manner.

CLAUDE SAMUEL.   Do you write quickly?

OLIVIER MESSIAEN.   Very quickly, when I'm started, and have the luck not to be interrupted. But I have a lot of trouble getting started; often it takes me a whole year, and it's in the summer, when the material has been accumulated, that I write quickly.

CLAUDE SAMUEL.   Do you make many corrections to this first sketch?

OLIVIER MESSIAEN.   I usually make three or four successive sketches, the last being an extremely well-written copy which I do not change again.

CLAUDE SAMUEL.   You don't, like some composers, touch up your old works?

OLIVIER MESSIAEN.   Oh no! Something finished is well and truly finished, and any alterations I might make a few years later wouldn't be in the same style: I would not be the same, I wouldn't have the same feelings, I would have developed.

CLAUDE SAMUEL.   Have you been tempted by transcriptions?

OLIVIER MESSIAEN.   Once only, and in the case of *L'Ascension*, which I originally wrote for orchestra and later transcribed for organ, the result was so troublesome that I had to recompose most of the pieces.

CLAUDE SAMUEL.   I was particularly alluding to works by other

99

composers that you could have transcribed: Schoenberg transcribing Bach chorale preludes, for example.

OLIVIER MESSIAEN.   No, such an idea never entered my head. I can see no use at all in this, unless it happens to be an academic task for learning orchestration.

CLAUDE SAMUEL.   Nevertheless, Ravel orchestrated Mussorgsky's "Pictures from an Exhibition".

OLIVIER MESSIAEN.   That is an absolutely sensational case of success, which is quite unique.

CLAUDE SAMUEL.   Finally, one must place to the credit of your creative work the texts you've written to introduce your works and which, in a way, illuminate your personality.

OLIVIER MESSIAEN.   I think those texts are important since, as you yourself say, they shed light on my works.

CLAUDE SAMUEL.   Do you conceive them as texts of purely didactic character or as rather free illustrations of the scores?

OLIVIER MESSIAEN.   These texts are intended to explain the form, technique and subject of my works; moreover, they are generally written in a French language which seeks to correspond with my musical language. It's for this last reason that they have sometimes caused surprise.

CLAUDE SAMUEL.   They certainly have surprised! But they, too, show this double aspect of your personality: technique allied to magic, and the meeting of the poet with the strict musician.

Conversation 6

CLAUDE SAMUEL. During the course of the preceding chapters we have spoken at length of your works and of your technical musical language; along the route, your artistic and human personality has slowly emerged. To narrow it further, I'd now like to ask you a few precise, even indiscreet, questions, having first confided to you that the impression your behaviour makes on me is that of a man at cross-purposes with his time. People bustle around you, millions of people in Paris, and hundreds of millions all over the world, and I won't say that these people worry you, but that you're unconcerned with them, you don't sense this bustle, you pass through it...

OLIVIER MESSIAEN. You're probably right and I'm probably in the wrong to be so; as a Christian, I should interest myself in everyone and love my neighbour. On the plane of friendship and affection, I hope to obey the precept—but I confess that the major preoccupations of my neighbour, my very close and actual neighbour, of any particular time, seem to me to be bizarre, absurd and quite distant from my own frame of mind.

CLAUDE SAMUEL. In other words, you're interested in your neighbour in his human depth; when you're in touch with him, he interests you because you wish perhaps to sound the depths of his being, but you're not at all concerned with his own preoccupations.

OLIVIER MESSIAEN. Exactly.

CLAUDE SAMUEL. And present-day civilisation doesn't interest you at all...

OLIVIER MESSIAEN. Oh... I'd say more: I'm near to detesting it!

CLAUDE SAMUEL. And what is your ideal civilisation, during which you would have liked to have lived?

OLIVIER MESSIAEN. I think of very old civilisations, for example, those of the Chaldeans, Sumerians or Hittites, those epochs where the word corresponded to reality, or the number was a symbol, where everything was taken seriously, where nothing was treated lightly, where correspondences were felt acutely.

CLAUDE SAMUEL. In short, you detest above all the frivolity of our time . . .

OLIVIER MESSIAEN. Its frivolity, its need of comfort which only makes it unhappy, and finally, it must be said, the escalation of war weapons which is particularly disquieting.

CLAUDE SAMUEL. But war is not only of today, and even during these dreamed-of civilisations to which you've just referred. . . .

OLIVIER MESSIAEN. Yes, of course, there have always been disputes to occupy the best place in the sun, but in the past one fought with lances or swords, which required bravery. Whereas today, there is no more bravery, and there are even no more heroes; quarrels, if they should take the course one fears, would end in almost total destruction.

CLAUDE SAMUEL. I know that this pacifist declaration bears no witness to any political engagement. This term "political engagement" is in complete contradiction to your personality.

OLIVIER MESSIAEN. I have a horror of politics. I've never been engaged in them, and I've a horror of being engaged by them. I'm a composer because I love music, and a Christian because I believe; but in this attitude there's no "engagement" at all.

CLAUDE SAMUEL. Yet, to a certain degree, to have the Catholic faith is an engagement and to believe in certain musical values constitutes another engagement.

OLIVIER MESSIAEN. Oh no! Because I'm persuaded that these things are true.

CLAUDE SAMUEL. Yes, but when one's engaged in a certain way, it's because one's persuaded that it's true. . . .

OLIVIER MESSIAEN. No, it's because one's persuaded that it's the best; there's a distinction there.

CLAUDE SAMUEL. So political engagement has never grazed your mind? Do you think that it's a useless thing?
OLIVIER MESSIAEN. Yes, absolutely.
CLAUDE SAMUEL. Because you're an artist?
OLIVIER MESSIAEN. No, this has nothing to do with artistic activity. It's a field which doesn't interest me.
CLAUDE SAMUEL. It seems to me that you also reproach our time for its very high technicality. You hardly appreciate our cars, airplanes, railways, factories, or machines of any kind.
OLIVIER MESSIAEN. No, technicality is useful, it's useful to the progress of mind and of humanity. What is troublesome in our epoch is that this technicality leads to catastrophes: to the destruction of true darkness, of true silence, to the destruction of true thought, to the intrusion into the heart of a peaceful family of musical noises that are unexpected and enforced whatever their style or aesthetic may be.
CLAUDE SAMUEL. To take concrete examples, you're not interested in such means of artistic and cultural diffusion as the radio, records or television?
OLIVIER MESSIAEN. But yes; I consider these things marvellous; they're absolutely inspired inventions which should have served to increase the artistic sense of the masses. Unfortunately, almost the contrary result has obtained.
CLAUDE SAMUEL. Would you adopt a position which would make one think of Jean-Jacques Rousseau?
OLIVIER MESSIAEN. Absolutely not. I've a horror of that writer. No, look, my chief reproach towards our epoch is its bad taste. All that surrounds us is made without taste. Man has covered the planet with his constructions, his towns and his buildings, all of which is obviously very functional and corresponds to commodities; only comfort doesn't prevent errors of shape and colour, maladjustment to the landscape, the absence of style and harmony, in a word—ugliness! Now, the Egyptians, Assyrians and the great builders and masters of stained-glass of the Roman and Gothic era considered something other than the functional aspect of a building; they saw in it a symbol, an elevation of the soul towards the Divinity, a manifestation of

103

the Divinity, in short, they saw in it what is invisible and what is truer than the visible; that's what we've lost.

CLAUDE SAMUEL. Nevertheless, despite the bad taste which characterises our epoch and the baneful aspects of technicality, aren't people happier than formerly?

OLIVIER MESSIAEN. Oh no! They are far less happy. You've only to walk in the street for five minutes to see screwed-up, severe and anguished looks, and never the least serenity.

CLAUDE SAMUEL. But don't you take any interest in the daring adventures of our time: the conquest of space and the arrival of men on the moon?

OLIVIER MESSIAEN. It's obviously extraordinary, but I really hope that after my death, without need of any equipment, I'll be able to get to planets far beyond our satellite and even in other solar systems.

CLAUDE SAMUEL. In short, you prefer to technical progress the internal mystery and magic which makes one dream. . . .

OLIVIER MESSIAEN. No, I prefer quite simply the Truths of the Faith which offers me everything at one go.

CLAUDE SAMUEL. I must admit that your attitude towards the conquests of our age astonish me all the more when, where artistic matters are concerned, you participate with passion in the building of a new world. In this new bivalence of your personality, don't you see some contradiction?

OLIVIER MESSIAEN. Not at all.

CLAUDE SAMUEL. Very well, let our readers pierce this other mystery and let's speak a little of a field where your taste for novelty was never in question: the field of teaching. For more than thirty years, you have taught daily, and this essential activity in the formation of a new musical school has, as much as your works, propagated your name throughout the whole world. For you, is teaching a natural function?

OLIVIER MESSIAEN. Yes, I adore teaching, and the day I retire and am deprived of my class I'll be extremely unhappy.

CLAUDE SAMUEL. Do you feel more the need to teach or the desire to live, day by day, in the company of young musicians?

OLIVIER MESSIAEN. It's rather complicated. I've always loved

104

analysis, the analysis of music in all its forms, and this responds to one of my main aspirations in musical work. Then, the fact of being surrounded by youngsters, youngsters who have confidence in me but who are very different from me, youngsters whom I have the duty not to thwart but to guide, each in his own path, is an excellent thing, for I'm getting on, like everyone, and this entourage helps to slow down the process. These youngsters are obviously more advanced than I am, but their questions and their attitude compels me to new researches of which I might not have dreamt without them.

CLAUDE SAMUEL. How would you characterise your teaching?

OLIVIER MESSIAEN. At the Conservatoire I have an Analysis Class*; the title is small but the actual thing is enormous, for this Analysis Class is really a "Super-Composition" Class, intended for young men and women from eighteen to twenty-eight who already have a considerable musical background. Most of them have obtained the highest awards in composition classes, sometimes a Grand Prix de Rome or a conducting prize or piano accompaniment prize. Some of them even have all these prizes together. So I address myself to some very remarkable musicians and I have to bring to them all that they haven't learnt in their previous classes, in particular all that the professors of those classes haven't had time to deal with. So, in the organ class, improvisation and organ playing have relegated to the back seat the study of neumes and of the rhythms of plainsong, which are nevertheless so useful to Catholic organists: so I do plainsong in my class. In composition classes, correction of pupils' works prevents professors from devoting much time to analysing works by the masters and also exotic, ancient and ultra-modern music: such analyses are the main work of my class. Always in composition classes, orchestration and instrumentation is dealt with too hurriedly: in my class we never stop talking about the possibilities of each instrument and the way to set out a page of orchestral score. Finally, the Paris Conservatoire, the provincial

* Since October, 1966, Olivier Messiaen has been in charge of a Composition Class at the Conservatoire.

105

conservatoires and I would even say all European and Western music schools, place the accent on harmony and counterpoint—there's never any question of rhythm: so I deal with rhythm in my class.

CLAUDE SAMUEL. But before directing this class, you taught outside the Conservatoire.

OLIVIER MESSIAEN. I took an ensemble class and a piano sight-reading class at the Ecole Normale de Musique from 1934 to 1939, then an improvisation class at the Schola, then a composition and orchestration course at Tanglewood (U.S.A.), courses in rhythm at Budapest, Sarrebrucken, Darmstadt and finally courses in Greek rhythms and the Indian deçî-tâlas at Buenos-Aires (Argentina) in 1963, quite apart from previous lecture-courses on music and ornithology at Winterthur (Switzerland), at Boulder (Colorado), then in Japan, Canada and in Finland. On the other hand, since 1942 I have been Harmony Professor at the Paris Conservatoire, but, concurrently with my harmony class, I gave a private course in the home of my friend the musicologist and composer Guy Bernard-Delapierre, and this was specifically an analysis course, analysis of form, orchestra, rhythm, melody, and harmony of all kinds of music: classical, romantic, ancient, exotic and modern. Having heard of the existence of this private course, the Director of the Conservatoire at the time, who was Claude Delvincourt, was excited by it; he judged this course to be of great interest and asked the Ministry to create a class comprising exactly the same work and the same elements. This request was granted and so the Analysis Class was founded.

CLAUDE SAMUEL. So now this is definitely established, it's not bound only to your person although you're actually its titular professor.

OLIVIER MESSIAEN. Alas, yes! For I do think that when I disappear it'll be rather difficult to find a successor. It's an extremely difficult and tiring class; imagine that each week I take three courses each of which lasts four hours, and that during these four hours I speak and give sometimes very difficult examples at the piano. To take this class, then, one needs a good voice, good and fluent spoken French, the ability to play the piano very well, to sight-read easily and to have a vast culture. But that isn't all, for here's the most terrible thing: the subject of the course changes each year. Obviously, I could always say the same things and sink into a rut, but students come to me because they know that they will stay two or three years in the class: even if they return as friends after having won their prize, they'll always hear something new. So each year we choose a subject; this year, for example, we've dealt with piano music. We started from the harpsichord with Couperin, Domenico Scarlatti and Rameau, then we studied practically all piano music, that is to say, the twenty-two concertos of Mozart, the thirty-two sonatas of Beethoven, nearly all the work of Chopin and Schumann, Albeniz's *Ibéria*, all Debussy's *Préludes, Estampes, Images* and *Etudes*, Ravel's *Gaspard de la nuit*, and we've even analysed Boulez's Second Sonata of which I've played bits.

CLAUDE SAMUEL.   This thrust towards the avant-garde, isn't it a revolution in an official Conservatoire?

OLIVIER MESSIAEN.   Everything I do is revolutionary. To analyse the twenty-two concertos of Mozart is a revolution, because it had never been spoken of in the rue de Madrid. . . .

CLAUDE SAMUEL.   Yes, but Mozart is all the same an "admitted" composer whereas the Conservatoire authorities could have protested against the modernist tendencies of your class.

OLIVIER MESSIAEN.   Claude Delvincourt was absolutely in agreement with the principles of my teaching. Since then, there have sometimes been protests, but with calm stubbornness I've stuck to my point of view and all has been well.

But I'm going to give you other examples of subjects chosen for my class. Two years ago, we dealt with opera: from Monteverdi's *Orfeo*, passing by way of the *opéra-ballet* of Rameau with *Castor et Pollux, Hippolyte et Aricie, Dardanus*, and *Platée*, to opera with airs and alternating recitatives, with Mozart's *Don Giovanni* which is the greatest of the type (an immortal masterpiece), continuing with *leitmotiv* opera with all Wagner's *Ring* (and I have spoken to my students not only of the *leitmotiv*, which I greatly admire in all its psychological, philosophical, cosmic, social and thaumaturgical resonances, but I procured, after long searches, the Eddas and Sagas which are the basis of the German text of the legend of the Nibelungs which Wagner used to write his poems); then we've looked at an opera with chorus—Mussorgsky's *Boris Godunov*—and then two modern operas, Debussy's *Pelléas et Mélisande* and Alban Berg's *Wozzeck*.

CLAUDE SAMUEL. These choices reflect your personal taste....

OLIVIER MESSIAEN. One can't deal with everything in a year. One chooses the best. But I've nevertheless wanted to deal with a repertory opera and opted for the one which appears to me the most striking and successful: Bizet's *Carmen*.

CLAUDE SAMUEL. But not Verdi, nor Puccini?

OLIVIER MESSIAEN. No, because we must restrict ourselves; in three terms, one can't study secondary works, one concentrates on masterpieces.

CLAUDE SAMUEL. In a general way, your taste intervenes to the extent that you don't take the trouble to analyse works which you don't like.

OLIVIER MESSIAEN. That depends. I don't tell my students where my preferences lie. This may transpire in my talks but, in principle, I seek to respect the opinion of my students and to divert them into paths which I think suit them.

CLAUDE SAMUEL. You said a moment ago: "During the course of the year, we have dealt with such and such an opera". What does this mean? How do you study a work?

OLIVIER MESSIAEN. We place its psychological climate, previous events that have influenced it and, in another sense, its posterity. For an opera, we are concerned with theatre, with the disposition of scenes, the division of the text, the orchestration, the instrumental forces, the vocal writing, the language of the composer (harmony, melodic lines, rhythmic system) and with form. In the theatre, form is obviously related to the dramatic movement, but we've spoken exclusively of those forms, and it was also very absorbing. I even reserved a year for *Rhythm*; it really was a revolution, much worse than speaking about

108

Boulez, and the greatest difficulty was getting members of the jury for the *Concours!* That year I spoke of the Gregorian Number or the rhythm of plainsong, of Mozartian accent, of Debussy's rhythmic undulation, of the rhythmic characters in Stravinsky's *Rite of Spring*, all this rounded off with a complete analysis of the Gânas, Karnatic theory, and the hundred and twenty deçî-tâlas of India, as well as initiation into Greek rhythm. It was a very fruitful year for the students, who were delighted. We also researched together into irrational note-values and polyrhythmic combinations of these values.

CLAUDE SAMUEL. But don't you ever choose the same theme twice in your courses?

OLIVIER MESSIAEN. After a certain time, I might be led to take up the same subject again, particularly if this subject proves of great interest, but there's no obligatory cycle and I avoid repetitions. I must also say that the theme of the year doesn't entirely depend on my whim, neither is it imposed on me. When I arrive on 1 October, I've some idea of it without being quite sure of my choice: it's the look on the faces of my students that decides it. This may appear very astonishing to you, but I'm a bit like a doctor or confessor: when I see my new students coming in, I examine them at length and say to myself: "This one needs such and such a remedy, or such and such a stimulant", and the year's subject will then be decided in sympathy with the characters facing me.

CLAUDE SAMUEL. Then, at this period of choice, there exists a dialogue, explicit or implicit, between students and professor, and I know that the dialogue continues. . . .

OLIVIER MESSIAEN. A very explicit dialogue, for, very often, towards 15 October, I say to my students: "Well then, given what you are, I intend to deal with such a subject this year; do you agree?" Some may protest. Perhaps one of them will say, "I'm a cellist, piano music doesn't interest me, I don't understand the fingering". Then I take account of the majority.

Throughout the whole academic year, I am seated at the piano: I play, and I speak (rather *ex cathedra*), but my words are often interrupted by the students' questions and there can be

109

some discussion between the students and myself, or even disputes between the students because they don't always agree: from these discussions spring light . . . and fellowship!

CLAUDE SAMUEL. So this class is a very autonomous and lively cell?

OLIVIER MESSIAEN. Extremely lively, because the personalities of the students are generally very varied and I seek with all my power to respect them.

CLAUDE SAMUEL. Are your students future composers?

OLIVIER MESSIAEN. In the main. Some are only instrumentalists wishing to perfect their musical instruction and some aim at musicology and wish to make their knowledge more complete.

CLAUDE SAMUEL. But do the composers bring you their first essays to be discussed together?

OLIVIER MESSIAEN. The task of correcting works is the role of the composition professors. I have no right to encroach on this field, but students who have followed my class for several years generally become friends and, when they've left the Conservatoire, if they submit their works to me—which often happens—certainly I look at them and try to give them advice.

CLAUDE SAMUEL. How large is your class?

OLIVIER MESSIAEN. Twenty strong at the maximum, fifteen French and five foreigners, divided among the two sexes with a majority of men.

CLAUDE SAMUEL. Do you think that among your student-composers, past or present, a rather clear common aesthetic line can be discerned?

OLIVIER MESSIAEN. No, they're all different. The glory of my class is precisely to respect personalities. I'm going to give you a precise and terrible example regarding Iannis Xenakis: when Iannis Xenakis came to find me, I had looked at him closely and found that he was an architect, a collaborator of Le Corbusier; I also learned that he was a mathematician. He asked me if he should bravely restart his musical studies at zero, enter a harmony class, then a fugue class, etc. . . . I reflected for some days and advised him against this, contrary to my musical predilections, and I encouraged him to use mathematics and

110

architecture in his music without preoccupying himself with problems of a melodico-harmonico-contrapuntico-rhythmico order. He followed this advice, which, it seems to me, has succeeded for him. However much his attitude may be reproached, it's nevertheless an extraordinary attitude in every sense of the term which brings a new stone to the musical building.

CLAUDE SAMUEL. Let's speak now of the outstanding personalities of your class, and, first of all, about the vanguard, those who were your disciples since the end of the war.

OLIVIER MESSIAEN. They've remained the most affectionate and the most important, and they're now the most famous—perhaps because they were the most gifted. In the very first place there's Pierre Boulez. He was so intelligent and such a musician that he had no need of a teacher; I'm convinced that he'd have done something splendid without any help. He worked a short time with me, just a year of harmony; he didn't join this famous analysis class. He gained his Harmony Prize at the first attempt, but he then took part in my private courses at Guy Bernard-Delapierre's.

CLAUDE SAMUEL. At a distance of twenty years, what does the Boulez phenomenon represent for you?

OLIVIER MESSIAEN. For me, Pierre Boulez is the greatest musician of his generation and, perhaps, of the half-century. He's also the greatest composer of serial music, I'd even say he was the only one. He is, moreover, in a certain sense, my successor in the field of rhythm. Pierre Boulez took from me the idea of rhythmic unease and the idea of rhythmic research, and also the use of certain formulas deriving directly from Greek and Indian rhythms, although in an unavowed manner. Despite this, he is very far from my musical universe.

CLAUDE SAMUEL. When you first knew Pierre Boulez, he was very young and in permanent and agressive revolt against a certain kind of music. . . .

OLIVIER MESSIAEN. He was in revolt against everything!

CLAUDE SAMUEL. Did you try to temper his anger?

OLIVIER MESSIAEN. I tried to communicate to him, if not a little

111

Faith and Charity, at least a little Hope: He's become much more human since that period. We came from a peaceful and conservative generation, and it was natural that, by reaction, one encountered rebels and eccentrics. And I think that such furies were fertile and resulted in a renewal of technique, asceticism and light.

CLAUDE SAMUEL. Don't you think that Pierre Boulez is, to a certain degree, at the Webern-Debussy junction?

OLIVIER MESSIAEN. He was very impressed by the aesthetic preoccupations of the Debussy of *Jeux* and the *Etudes*. This reaction is completely personal to him, for that's not the Debussy I prefer. For me, the great Debussy remains the *Nocturnes* and *Pelléas*.

CLAUDE SAMUEL. It appears then that you're in aesthetic contradiction with Pierre Boulez. . . .

OLIVIER MESSIAEN. But I'm in contradiction with all my pupils, that's exactly why my class is so lively! Moreover, it's quite normal that an older teacher should be in contradiction with younger pupils, the question of age should not be forgotten: to the aesthetic conflict is added the conflict of generation.

CLAUDE SAMUEL. Let's return to the students of those early days, to the colleagues of Pierre Boulez. . . .

OLIVIER MESSIAEN. Beside Pierre Boulez there was an obviously inspired person, Yvonne Loriod. She was also my pupil, my first pupil. She was gifted in everything: already at that time she was an extraordinary pianist; but she was also marvellously gifted at harmony, composition, rhythm and poetry.

CLAUDE SAMUEL. And then, around these exceptional personalities, there were a certain number of composers.

OLIVIER MESSIAEN. There was Maurice Le Roux who was passionately devoted to music; he too was gifted at everything. There was Serge Nigg, who went in several directions; I liked Serge Nigg, who was one of my greatest hopes. . . .

CLAUDE SAMUEL. You aren't worried by the frequent aesthetic variations of this composer?

OLIVIER MESSIAEN. I can say nothing: that is how his personality is. Certain characters follow a very straight and flashing path, they take off like arrows; others zig-zag. The essential thing is to reach the objective. Again, I may mention Jean-Louis Martinet who already had a fine technique, Michel Fano who turned towards the cinema but who was a very good musician, and finally Jean Barraqué, a rebel of the Boulez type, although in a different way, as his works show.

CLAUDE SAMUEL. In your album of memories, there's surely a place for your foreign pupils. . . .

OLIVIER MESSIAEN. Among the foreigners, the most important is obviously the great and inspired Karlheinz Stockhausen, who was in my class at the time I was dealing with Mozart's accentuations. And then I've had many Japanese: Sadao Bekku, who's a composer, critic and teacher in Tokyo; Mitsuaki Hayama, also well-known as a composer in Japan; and Shinohara, who's at the extreme point of the avant-garde. Among the Chinese, I need only name an exquisite highly cultivated man, the composer Chang Hao. Finally, I really must speak of some very remarkable recent pupils. The first was Raffi Ourgandjian, a musician of Armenian origin, who is an extraordinary improviser at the organ and also an admirable composer; in the field of rhythm, notably in the study of Indian rhythms, he is perhaps my only true disciple. I've had other pupils who are extraordinary creatures and I think that three major personalities must be cited in the first place: Gilbert Amy, who is now very well known as one of the best serialists; then two musicians of the same generation, very different from each other: Jean-Pierre Guézec and Paul Méfano. The first is soft-grained, a scrupulously careful and sensitive seeker whose works align extremely refined rhythms and colours; as for Méfano, he's another rebel, but a boiling and powerful rebel, a kind of twentieth-century Berlioz, with all the technical know-how, all the daring of language, and all the power of imagination and of realisation that this comparison calls for.

CLAUDE SAMUEL. And you love your rebel pupils?

OLIVIER MESSIAEN. I love them all, whether they be gentle, soft-grained, furious, rebellious or pacific!

Conversation 7

CLAUDE SAMUEL.   During the course of our conversations, we have often evoked the currents of present-day music in speaking of your work, your pupils and your admirations; we could now, in the form of a coda at the end of these conversations, ask ourselves about the essence of this modern music, about the evolution of the art of sounds, about this kind of rupture that some denounce today. Do you accept this term, "rupture"?

OLIVIER MESSIAEN.   Certainly not. The music of our time continues very normally the music of the past; without doubt there are changes, but no "rupture".

CLAUDE SAMUEL.   No "rupture", but perhaps an acceleration in evolution?

OLIVIER MESSIAEN.   In this, music follows the general movement of humanity that has found and made a thousand times more things during the past fifty years than it had found and made during all its previous existence on our planet.

CLAUDE SAMUEL.   But what appears normal in the technical order doesn't seem so obvious in an artistic field.

OLIVIER MESSIAEN.   It's not obvious but it's a fact.

CLAUDE SAMUEL.   Isn't it an optical illusion for us who live in this period, and won't our great grand-children think quite differently?

OLIVIER MESSIAEN.   No, it's quite clear: there have been many more changes and discoveries in the twentieth century than in all the preceding centuries since the coming of Christ.

CLAUDE SAMUEL.   And on the musical plane?

OLIVIER MESSIAEN.   We are witnessing a great upheaval, an upheaval without doubt as radical as that which occurred in the Middle Ages between the essentially melodic plainsong and the progressive discovery of counterpoint which necessitated the blend of several voices; the other change was proportional notation which allowed rhythmic combinations. The change today is almost of the same order, it's obviously very serious but not without a link with the past. The people of the Middle Ages preserved with the past the link of melody; as for us, we have all the same the link of harmonic control and of the ear's control over timbre.

CLAUDE SAMUEL. In your view, who are largely responsible for the speedy evolutionary process of modern music?

OLIVIER MESSIAEN. In the very first place, Debussy, who introduced the idea of haziness, not only in harmony and melody but above all in rhythm and in the succession of timbres. After him came Schoenberg, who was not perhaps a great composer but who was, at least, a great destroyer; and, in a sense, this destruction was useful because it allowed for the rejection of tonal barriers before leading to the discovery of the series.

CLAUDE SAMUEL. Your sensitivity separates you rather from the work of Schoenberg?

OLIVIER MESSIAEN. I admit that Schoenberg is not a composer I like more than any other.

CLAUDE SAMUEL. On the other hand, how do you place yourself in relation to Schoenberg's two great disciples: Berg and Webern?

OLIVIER MESSIAEN. Well, I too would say that they're "two great disciples". For me, serial music found its zenith with Pierre Boulez. He is the great serial composer, because he has mastered and gone beyond this language instead of becoming enslaved by it.

CLAUDE SAMUEL. And yet, Webern comes very precisely at the turning-point of this evolution.

OLIVIER MESSIAEN. Quite so. Webern was the "real" serial composer; Schoenberg and Berg were the precursors, and Boulez is both the realiser and the "outstepper".

CLAUDE SAMUEL. Among the pioneers of the new art, the names

of some other composers should be inscribed; and first I would mention as a reminder Igor Stravinsky. . . .

OLIVIER MESSIAEN. Stravinsky is of immense importance because he was the first to replace the accent on *Rhythm*: by the use of solely rhythmic themes, superimposed rhythmic ostinati, and above all in creating (consciously or unconsciously) the process of "rhythmic characters". This last process follows, by amplifying it, the Beethovenian type of development or "development by elimination". *The Glorification of the Chosen One* and even more the *Ritual Dance* of *The Rite of Spring* are striking examples of juxtaposition and movements by augmentation, diminution or immobility of "rhythmic characters".

CLAUDE SAMUEL. But isn't it deceptive to find in the work of Stravinsky, after this formidable invention which you yourself have called attention to in *The Rite of Spring*, a kind of going back, a disquieting serrated trajectory?

OLIVIER MESSIAEN. It is, I admit, inexplicable.

CLAUDE SAMUEL. In the line of pioneers, we should also place a composer who is less famous but no less important: Edgar Varèse.

OLIVIER MESSIAEN. Varèse is very important, for he foreshadowed the procedures of *musique concrète* and electronic music. He was the first to "pass" sounds backwards, without any apparatus or manipulation, by simply notating them on manuscript-paper. For example, in *Intégrales* he wrote trombone sounds which begin with the extinction of sound, swell and end with the attack. His rethought harmony (where the concept of chord is replaced by complexes of resonances calculated to produce maximum colour and intensity) is equally prophetic of most of the sonorities of today. . . .

CLAUDE SAMUEL. Do you think that with these few names, Debussy, Schoenberg, Berg and Webern on the one hand, and Stravinsky and Varèse on the other, we've done the round, without any serious omission, of those responsible for the new art?

OLIVIER MESSIAEN. Not entirely. One should all the same add

beside Varèse the name of André Jolivet, who is his continuation and who also brought his stone to the building, notably by returning magic to music. This incantatory aspect is certainly not to be disdained: the psychic, physiological and perhaps therapeutic action of a work like the *Danses rituelles* is still not understood: it's still a little known power.

CLAUDE SAMUEL. Alongside these pioneers other composers have adopted fruitful and very characteristic paths while still giving birth sometimes to true masterpieces. I think at first of personalities like Bartók and Falla whose steps in the direction of folklore are rather far from your own preoccupations.

OLIVIER MESSIAEN. Yes, they are composers who have had their hour, great composers. You can also add a composer who, because he was so prolific, was more "mixed", a composer who played an essential role: Villa Lobos.

CLAUDE SAMUEL. I know that you have an affection for this composer because he was a great orchestrator.

OLIVIER MESSIAEN. A very great orchestrator!

CLAUDE SAMUEL. But I'd like to return to the case of Bartók, who in the eyes of many music-lovers represents the gate opening on to modern music.

OLIVIER MESSIAEN. Bartók is a mixture of Hungarian folk-music, very special, very original, but rather academic developments after the manner of fugal episodes, and a tendency towards an increasingly close-knit chromaticism, very near to serial music.

CLAUDE SAMUEL. But aren't you sensitive to the fact that Bartók loved to travel through the countryside to collect folksongs and that, in his way, like you he interrogated nature?

OLIVIER MESSIAEN. Yes, but his quest was very different. It wasn't nature that he sought, but men. It must be said that his effort was rewarded because Hungarian folksong is among the world's liveliest, most varied, and most original. To me it only seems surpassed by the folksongs of the Andes, that is to say, those of Peru, Bolivia and Ecuador.

CLAUDE SAMUEL. Assuredly you prefer "exotic" music to that of folksong character.

OLIVIER MESSIAEN. "Exotic" music has played a great part in my own music, and also in that of Pierre Boulez, who was enthusiastic about Balinese and native African music. Something of this has remained with him; there's the obvious influence of exotic instrumentation in *Le Marteau sans maître*.

CLAUDE SAMUEL. And you think that a Western composer can find a lesson in these very ancient musical traditions coming from very distant continents?

OLIVIER MESSIAEN. Certainly, because the composers of those countries know things of which we are ignorant; they have made studies in rhythm which we have neglected in error. Finally, internationalism is one of the hallmarks of our time.

CLAUDE SAMUEL. Would it be sound to tie up the phenomenon of jazz with these discoveries of folk or exotic music?

OLIVIER MESSIAEN. Personally, I've never had an affection for jazz. I'm sorry to say it, but I think that jazz is a "robber" whose "innovations" are, really, borrowing from previous symphonic music.

CLAUDE SAMUEL. You appear to be severe in opposition to an art which represents, all the same, the creation of a new phenomenon.

OLIVIER MESSIAEN. Perhaps, but, in order to judge, I ought to have heard some real jazz.

CLAUDE SAMUEL. You know that some "classical" composers, indeed more or less serial, approach jazz to try to create a new music. You know, for example, the attempts by André Hodeir and you know also that in the United States a composer like Gunther Schuller follows the same path. Don't you think that these steps are viable?

OLIVIER MESSIAEN. I don't know. I've never believed in jazz and I've always thought that the poetic and refined figure of Maurice Ravel was spoilt in his last years by this influence of jazz, which really had nothing to do with his personal tendencies.

CLAUDE SAMUEL. And little to do with real jazz! But, since we're evoking some tendencies which have influenced certain composers between the two wars, I'd like to know your opinion of "neo-classicism"?

OLIVIER MESSIAEN. It's a very strange phenomenon, inexplicable and curiously unique. Previously there had never been any of these spectacular returns to past centuries. The Renaissance itself was a re-creation and not a useless copy....

CLAUDE SAMUEL. Do you know any valuable works which have been instigated by the neo-classical movement?

OLIVIER MESSIAEN. Ah, no! The principle is totally damnable; I'd even say it's completely absurd.

CLAUDE SAMUEL. Then let's forget all these whirlpools of Western musical life which the war of 1939 swept away. 1945 was the beginning of a new era, the blossoming of all these tendencies that were being developed for more than forty years despite sarcasms and which had to find their fulfilment in a certain number of new musical and important events. For us these events began with the *Domaine Musical*.

OLIVIER MESSIAEN. *Le Domaine Musical* represents the effort of one man, Pierre Boulez, not only to present serial aesthetic and his own theories, but also to get a whole group of contemporary composers accepted. It's a unique effort and very extraordinary because it's the work of a man whose courage and lucidity are linked with a marvellous technique, and answer most of our problems at one go.

Le Domaine Musical also represents the place where one is sure of hearing all the works of value coming from all over the world (the very good ones like the less good—especially the very good!) and even so it's pleasant to know that we have in Paris a kind of melting-pot from which masterpieces occasionally emerge.

CLAUDE SAMUEL. When you're in Paris, you never miss a concert of the *Domaine Musical*?

OLIVIER MESSIAEN. I've had my regular box for years.

CLAUDE SAMUEL. Which are the centres of modern music that have impressed you?

OLIVIER MESSIAEN. On a scale analogous to the *Domaine Musical*, there's Darmstadt and the Festival of

Donaueschingen. But many festivals of modern music have been born more recently: Warsaw, which is the extreme point of the avant-garde, Venice, Royan, Saint-Paul-de-Vence, Thonon-les-Bains. . . .

CLAUDE SAMUEL. So much for the frame. This frame is peopled by many composers who, for the most part, belong more or less to the serial aesthetic. Do you think that the strongest current in the music of today is serial music?

OLIVIER MESSIAEN. It's a current, but not the only one. I can see at least one other, equally important, which embodies the music called "electronic" and its elder sister, *musique concrète*; and there we must all the same mention the name of Pierre Schaeffer at which so many people cast stones, forgetting that he was a greater discoverer of new sonorities (without forgetting his successor, Pierre Henry).

CLAUDE SAMUEL. Have you been tempted by *musique concrète* or by electronic music?

OLIVIER MESSIAEN. I didn't have a gift for it. Once, I wrote a piece of *musique concrète*: it was very bad. "Concrete" and "electronic" music have given us really extraordinary timbres as well as a new conception of time and of sonorous space. Now, it's indeed possible to recapture their processes quite simply with orchestral instruments: that's the direction of certain works by Xenakis and Penderecki.

CLAUDE SAMUEL. Do you think that one day electronic music will supplant instrumental music?

OLIVIER MESSIAEN. One might have thought so when it was first invented, but today it may be seen that results quite as new and valid have been obtained from conventional instruments; in consequence, it's likely that these two kinds of music will co-exist, as can the cinema and the theatre.

CLAUDE SAMUEL. Has electronic music already produced masterpieces?

OLIVIER MESSIAEN. No, and more's the pity! It's produced above all experimental works.

CLAUDE SAMUEL. After the serial current, after the electronic and concrete current, the "mathematical" current must be

121

considered—its most significant representative is Iannis Xenakis—or yet other experiments which tend to add an electronic computer to the composer's task. Isn't your affectionate feeling for nature repelled by this idea of an electronic brain associated with a creator?

OLIVIER MESSIAEN. I admit that it would never occur to me to pose a question to an electronic brain, first of all because I'd be incapable; I also think that the questioned electronic brain would very quickly produce thousands, if not millions, of answers, and, among these thousands or millions of answers, there's only one that may be right. Rather than trouble an extremely burdened apparatus and spend months in formulating a question, isn't it quicker to have genius and to find the right answer right away? Having said that, I don't utterly condemn the steps taken by Xenakis, whom I admire profoundly. It's a very special direction but quite in keeping with our age, for the introduction of mathematics and the sciences into music is a reflection of our time, almost necessary and even inevitable.

CLAUDE SAMUEL. But some people wonder whether the introduction of calculus doesn't imply the supression of sensitivity.

OLIVIER MESSIAEN. No, not at all. It's a way of working which in no way hinders the realisation of a work which may be beautiful, noble and expressive (taking these three adjectives in a broad sense).

Moreover, analysis, synthesis and the science of numbers are closely related to music. Only the theory of groups can take into account the great "musical noises" of nature: storms, waterfalls, and the complex sounds of wind and sea. In music we lacked the theory of groups and its working outcome: the Calculus of probability. Let's thank Iannis Xenakis for having given them to us!

CLAUDE SAMUEL. What do you feel when listening to the works of Xenakis? Do you think of the Calculus?

OLIVIER MESSIAEN. Certainly not. I receive the shock produced by the sounds, by the calculated difference of tempi, the

122

different glissandi and the clouds of pizzicati, etc. . . .

CLAUDE SAMUEL. Do you believe that Xenakis is actually opening a door through which many composers could come to grief?

OLIVIER MESSIAEN. It's extremely likely.

CLAUDE SAMUEL. Another innovation: the use of chance, or rather of "aleatory". This school was first launched in the United States by composers such as John Cage and Earl Brown, but many composers, some as famous as Boulez and Stockhausen, have, in their own way, plumbed "aleatory". What do you think of it?

OLIVIER MESSIAEN. These attempts should be considered with caution; that, moreover is the attitude of Pierre Boulez. Personally, I don't believe in chance. Nor does Xenakis believe in it since he calculates it: a calculated chance isn't a chance! I don't believe in chance because I'm a Christian; I believe in Providence and I think that all that happens is foreseen. Certainly the freedom of events is respected but, for God who sees everything simultaneously, there's no chance. Further, I think that in art there is *one* truth, *one* version that is good, a choice which is operated automatically by genius. . . .

A flower, from which an insect takes pollen to spread abroad, is doubtless going to engender another flower; but it's sent away a quantity of pollen capable of producing thousands of flowers; nevertheless, one alone will result from insemination by the legs of the insect. . . .

I would add one last statement which is very serious: it's unthinkable that man, who by his very nature has only a fragmentary and, above all, successive view of things, could conceive all the possibilities and their consequences of no matter what subject: that belongs to God alone.

CLAUDE SAMUEL. In regard to all the currents which we've just discussed—aleatory, concrete and electronic music—one is accustomed to use the term "experimental". Isn't this word in contradiction to the necessary fulfilment of a work of art? Is this an error of terminology? Do you think that, in past centuries, certain works could also be classed in this denomination?

123

OLIVIER MESSIAEN. All aesthetic research is an experiment, inevitably. It's a simple error to use this term in a pejorative sense, and, again, work doesn't prevent success.

CLAUDE SAMUEL. Yet this accumulation of "experiments" actually results in musical forms of extreme complexity, both for the listener and for the executant. Where will this ever-increasing complexity lead us?

OLIVIER MESSIAEN. The works of the past, too, appeared very difficult to perform and still more difficult to listen to when they were created: then virtuosos progressed, technique evolved, ears became accustomed and hearing was modified. A similar result will be reached by the music of the twentieth century.

CLAUDE SAMUEL. Do you imagine that, in thirty or forty years' time, the public will accept works which appear to us most difficult, just as today we accept *Pelléas et Mélisande*?

OLIVIER MESSIAEN. Very probably.

CLAUDE SAMUEL. And that day when the average music-lover will be able to play the Third Sonata of Boulez like the Chopin *Préludes*, what music will the young composers be writing? How many puzzles will have to be solved? How will the art of the future release itself from the formidable ebullience of the present time?

OLIVIER MESSIAEN. No one has a right to speak of the future, and I would be the last to want to play the prophet. I can only affirm that the different currents which we've just examined have served to enrich the world of sound greatly and have provoked a kind of fusion of the old melodic-harmonic division (a fusion of the vertical and the horizontal), but above all—and I think that this is where their major contribution lies, for we are creatures living in time—they have imposed a new concept of time.

Chronology

1908 Dec 10   Olivier Messiaen born at Avignon, where his father, Pierre Messiaen, a translator of Shakespeare, was an English teacher. His mother, the poetess Cécile Sauvage, had just written *L'Ame en bourgeon*, dedicated to the son about to be born.

1914   On the mobilisation of his father, Olivier Messiaen and his mother went to live in Grenoble.

1918   First music lessons in Nantes.

1919   Enters Paris Conservatoire (Professors: Jean and Nöel Gallon, Georges Caussade, Estyle, Marcel Dupré, Maurice Emmanuel and Paul Dukas.

1925   *Premier Prix* for counterpoint and fugue.

1927   *Premier Prix* for piano accompaniment.

1929   *Premiers Prix* for organ, improvisation, and History of Music. *Préludes* for piano.

1930   *Premier Prix* for composition. End of his studies at the Conservatoire.

1931   Olivier Messiaen appointed organist at the church of the Sainte-Trinité.

       Feb 19   First performance of *Les Offrandes oubliées* at the Théâtre des Champs-Elysées under Walter Straram.

1935   *La Nativité du Seigneur*, nine meditations for organ.

1936		Founding of the *Jeune France* group, comprising Olivier Messiaen, André Jolivet, Daniel-Lesur and Yves Baudrier.
		Olivier Messiaen is appointed Professor at the Ecole Normale de Paris and at the Schola Cantorum.
		Poèmes pour Mi, for voice and piano.
1938		*Chants de Terre et de Ciel*, for voice and piano.
1939		*Les Corps Glorieux*, for organ.
		Olivier Messiaen mobilised as a Private.
1940	June	Olivier Messiaen taken prisoner.
1941	Jan 15	The *Quatuor pour la fin du Temps*, for violin, clarinet, cello and piano, composed in Stalag 8 A in Silesia, performed to an audience of 5,000 prisoners.
1942		On his return to Paris, Olivier Messiaen is appointed Professor of Harmony at the Conservatoire.
1943	May 10	First performance of the *Visions de l'Amen* for two pianos at the Concerts de la Pléiade by Yvonne Loriod and the composer.
1943—1947		Composition classes at the home of Guy Bernard-Delapierre.
1944		*Technique de mon langage musical*.
1945	Mar 26	Yvonne Loriod gives the first performance, at the Salle Gaveau, of the *Vingt Regards sur l'Enfant Jésus*.
	Apr 21	Roger Désormière conducts at the Concert de la Pléiade the first performance of the *Trois Petites Liturgies de la Présence Divine*.
1947		An Analysis Class, created for the purpose at the Paris Conservatoire, is entrusted by Claude Delvincourt to Olivier Messiaen.

Course in musical analysis at the Budapest Conservatoire.

1948   Tour in Italy organised by Luigi Dallapiccola.

1949   Course in composition at the Berkshire Music Center at Tanglewood (U.S.A.).

Cinq Rechants for mixed choir of twelve voices a cappella.

Dec 2   First performance at Boston of the Turangalîla-Symphonie conducted by Leonard Bernstein. The score, commissioned by Serge Koussevitzky and the Koussevitzky Foundation for the Boston Symphony Orchestra, was composed between July 17, 1946 and November 29, 1948.

1950   Messe de la Pentecôte for organ.

Course in rhythmic analysis at Darmstadt.

1951   Livre d'Orgue. This work, first performed by the composer at Stuttgart in 1953, was also played by him on November 21, 1955, at the church of the Sainte-Trinité, in Paris.

1953   Le Réveil des oiseaux for piano and orchestra.

Course in rhythmic analysis at Sarrebrucken.

1955   Oiseaux exotiques, for piano solo, two clarinets, wind chamber orchestra, xylophone, glockenspiel and percussion.

1959 Apr 15   First performance by Yvonne Loriod at the concerts of the Domaine Musical of the Catalogue d'Oiseaux for piano.

1960   Chronochromie for orchestra.

1962   Visit to Japan with Yvonne Loriod.

Seiji Ozawa conducts the Turangalîla-Symphonie in Tokyo. Sept Haïkaï, Japanese sketches, for piano

127

solo, xylophone and marimba soli, two clarinets, one trumpet and small orchestra (first performance: October 30, 1963, conducted by Pierre Boulez at the Domaine Musical).

1963	Dec	Visit to Sofia where Constantin Iliev conducts the *Turangalîla-Symphonie.*
1964		Visit to the Argentine and course in rhythm at Buenos Aires.
	Oct 17	First performance, at the Donaueschingen Festival under Pierre Boulez, of *Couleurs de la Cité celeste* for piano solo, 3 clarinets, 3 xylos, brass ensemble and metallic percussion.
1965	May 7	Private first performance at the Sainte-Chapelle in Paris of *Et exspecto resurrectionem mortuorum* conducted by Serge Baudo.
	June 20	Repeated in Chartres Cathedral, in the presence of Général de Gaulle.
1966	Jan 12	First public performance of *Et exspecto resurrectionem mortuorum* at the Domaine Musical under Pierre Boulez.
	May	Visit to Finland.
	Oct	Olivier Messiaen appointed Composition Professor at the Paris Conservatoire.
1967		Messiaen week at Thonon.
		Olivier Messiaen *Concours de piano* at the Royan Festival.

Chronology since 1967
especially compiled by the composer for this
English edition

1967	Jan 30	Olivier Messiaen Festival in Paris, Palais de Chaillot.

Feb	Messiaen Week in Thonon.
Mar	First *Concours de piano* "Olivier Messiaen" for contemporary music at Royan (First Prize winner: Michel Beroff).
Apr 22	*Turangalîla-Symphonie* at Hilversum.
June	*Chronochromie* at Tokyo.
Dec 5—6	*Turangalîla-Symphonie* at Toronto (Conductor: Seiji Ozawa).
Dec	Tour in U.S.A.
Dec 20	Election by unanimous vote to the Institut de France, Académie des Beaux Arts.
1968 Feb 6—10	*Et exspecto resurrectionem mortuorum* in Paris and Bourges.
Mar 12	*Turangalîla-Symphonie* in Liverpool.
Mar	Second *Concours de piano* "Olivier Messiaen" at Royan (First Prize winner: Jean-Rodolphe Kars).
Jul 4—6	English Bach Festival in London.
	Vingt Regards, Turangalîla-Symphonie, L'Ascension, Et exspecto.
Dec 4—8	Messiaen Week at Düsseldorf (for Messiaen's 60th birthday) organised by Mme. Almut Rössler who played the complete organ works.
	Orchestral works conducted by Oskar Gottlieb Blarr.
1969 Jan/Feb	Tour in France with *Le Réveil des Oiseaux*.
Feb 5, 6, 8	*Turangalîla-Symphonie* in Brussels.
Mar	Third *Concours de piano* "Olivier Messiaen" at Royan (First Prize winner: Catherine Collard).

129

May 5	*Turangalîla-Symphonie* in Belgrade.
1965—1969	Composition and orchestration of *La Transfiguration de Notre Seigneur Jésus-Christ* for choir, seven instrumental soloists and large orchestra.
June 7	First Performance in Lisbon, Portugal, of *La Transfiguration de Notre Seigneur Jésus-Christ*, at the Coliseu, before an audience of 9000. Orchestre de Paris, Conductor: Serge Baudo; Piano Solo: Yvonne Loriod; Cello Solo: Mstislav Rostropovitch. (Work commissioned by Madame M. de Azeredo de Perdigao for the Gulbenkian Foundation.)
Sep	Journey to Persepolis, Iran, with Yvonne Loriod.
	Et exspecto conducted by Bruno Maderna. Visit to the Tombs of the Kings, the Kings Akhemenides and the Tomb of Cyrus at Pasargarde.
Sep 13	*Trois petites Liturgies* at Ghent, for the Flanders Festival.
Oct 20	Messiaen Day at the Paris S.M.I.P. *Catalogue d'Oiseaux* (Yvonne Loriod), *Quatuor pour la fin du Temps*, *Livre d'Orgue* (Raffi Ourgandjian).
Oct 20, 21, 22, 25	*La Transfiguration de notre Seigneur Jésus-Christ* (first performance in France).
1970 Mar	Fourth *Concours de piano "Olivier Messiaen"* at Royan (First Prize winner: Maria-Elena Barrientos).
May 30	*Turangalîla-Symphonie* at Rome (Conductor: Seiji Ozawa).
Jul 7	*La Transfiguration* in London (BBC Symphony Orchestra and Choir; Conductor; Serge Baudo).
Summer	Composition of *La Fauvette des jardins* for piano.
Oct/Nov	Tour in the U.S.A. and Canada: Hanover, Calgary,

Santa Barbara, Berkeley, Pasadena. Vancouver, New York, Quebec: *Le Réveil des Oiseaux*, *Chronochromie* (27—28 October, conducted by Pierre Dervaux—Ottawa), Boston, Yellow Spring, Montreal, Washington D.C.

Dec 11—13	*La Transfiguration* at Liége.

1971 Feb   Messiaen Week at Rennes.

Apr   Fifth *Concours de piano* "Olivier Messiaen" at Royan (First Prize winners: Hakon Austbö and Pierre Réach).

May   Maggio musicale at Florence, Messiaen Festival (Conductor: Roger Albin).

end of May   Filming of Mme. Denise Tual's "Olivier Messiaen et les oiseaux".

May 30   Death of Marcel Dupré (Olivier Messiaen's teacher).

June 10, 11, 12   *La Transfiguration* at Munich (Conductor: Rafaël Kubelik).

June 25   Reception for the award of the Erasmus Prize at Amsterdam, given by Queen Juliana and Prince Bernhard.

Summer   Began *Des Canyons aux étoiles...*, which will occupy him until 1974.

Oct 9   Reception for the award of the Sibelius Prize in Helsinki.

Dec 19   *Oiseaux exotiques* at the Espace Pierre Cardin in Paris (Conductor: Daniel Chabrun, Piano solo: Yvonne Loriod).

1972 Mar   Tour in the U.S.A.

Mar 20   First performance of the *Méditations sur le Mystère de la Sainte-Trinité* for organ by the composer at the National Shrine of the Immaculate Conception in Washington (before an audience of 3,500).

131

Olivier Messiaen made Doctor *honoris causa* of the Catholic University of the U.S.A.

Mar 28, 29, 30	First performance in the U.S.A. of *La Transfiguration*, conducted by Antal Dorati, Washington National Orchestra, Princeton Choir, Yvonne Loriod (piano solo), at the Kennedy Center.
Apr 2	*La Transfiguration* at New York, Carnegie Hall (Easter Sunday). Continuation of U.S.A. tour: New York, Appleton (Wisconsin), Berkeley, Pasadena.
Apr 28, 29	Recording of *La Transfiguration* in Washington for Decca. Visit to Utah with Yvonne Loriod: Bryce Canyon, Cedar Breaks, Zion Park.
May 12	*Et exspecto* at Los Angeles (Conductor: Zubin Mehta).
June	Messiaen Week at Düsseldorf: Complete organ works including the first European performance of the *Méditations sur le Mystère de la Sainte-Trinité* by Almut Rössler, *Visions de l'Amen* (Olivier Messiaen and Yvonne Loriod), *Et exspecto* and *Couleurs de la Cité céleste* (Conductor: O. G. Blarr).
Sept 22	*Turangalîla-Symphonie* at Brno (Conductor: Daniel Sternefeld).
Nov 7	First performance of *La Fauvette des jardins* by Yvonne Loriod at the Espace Pierre Cardin in Paris with the *Sept Haïkaï* and *Et exspecto* (Conductor: Marius Constant).
Dec 12	Marseilles, and
Dec 14	Toulouse: *Visions de l'Amen* played for the 150th time by Yvonne Loriod and Olivier Messiaen.
1973 Feb 17—21	Messiaen Week at Chalon sur Saône: *Harawi*,

Oiseaux exotiques, La Fauvette des jardins, Catalogue d'Oiseaux, Vingt Regards, Visions de l'Amen.

Mar 13   Messiaen Week at Cardiff: *Oiseaux exotiques*, organ pieces by Gillian Weir, *Quatuor, Visions de l'Amen* (Yvonne Loriod and Olivier Messiaen).

Mar 29—30   *Turangalîla-Symphonie* at Rotterdam (Conductor; Jean Fournet).

Apr 8   First performance of *La Fauvette des jardins* in Italy at Perugia, *Vingt Regards* by Yvonne Loriod.

Apr   Sixth *Concours de Piano* "Olivier Messiaen", at La Rochelle (First Prize winner: Pierre-Laurent Aimard, aged 15).

Apr   Messiaen Week in London (English Bach Festival):

Apr 24   First performance in England of *La Fauvette des jardins* by Yvonne Loriod, *Visions de l'Amen* by Yvonne Loriod and Olivier Messiaen.

Apr 27   *La Transfiguration* at St. Paul's Cathedral (Conductor: Marius Constant).

Complete organ works by five organists, including the *Méditations sur le Mystère de la Sainte-Trinité* by Almut Rössler on 2 May.

May 3   *Et exspecto* in Westminster Cathedral (Conductor: Marius Constant).

May 29—30   *Chronochromie* at Angers and Nantes (Conductor: Pierre Dervaux).

May   Nomination: Member of the Academy San Fernando, Madrid.

Nomination: Member of the Academy of Arts and Sciences, Boston (Mass.)

June 9   *La Transfiguration* at Vienna (Conductor: Miltiades Caridis).

June	Messiaen Week at Flanders Festival, Tongeren: First performance in Belgium of the *Méditations* by Almut Rössler; *La Fauvette* and *Vingt Regards* by Yvonne Loriod, and, at Hasselt, *Turangalîla-Symphonie* (Conductor: Daniel Sternefeld).
June 23	*L'Ascension, Le Réveil des Oiseaux* and *Chronochromie* at Amsterdam (Conductor: Jean Fournet).
Oct	Tour in the U.S.A.: 18 and 20 October: *Turangalîla-Symphonie* at Cleveland (Conductor: Louis Lane); two Messiaen days at Minneapolis: *Vingt Regards, Visions de l'Amen, Oiseaux exotiques, Cinq Rechants, Quatuor,* three Messiaen days in New York: *Vingt de l'Amen, Quatuor, Trois Petites Liturgies.* Messiaen Week in Mount Vernon, Iowa: *Messe de la Pentecôte* (by Clyde Holloway), *Quatuor, Vingt Regards, Visions de l'Amen.* Olivier Messiaen elected D.Litt. of Cornell College (Iowa). Continuation of tour: Ithaca. Hanover: *Vingt Regards* (by Peter Serkin), first U.S.A. performance of *La Fauvette des jardins* (by Yvonne Loriod), Lecture on Olivier Messiaen (by Felix Aprahamian), *Visions de l'Amen* (by Yvonne Loriod and Olivier Messiaen) at Dartmouth College.
Nov 24—27	*Vingt Regards* and *Visions de l'Amen* at Metz Festival; organ *Méditations, Oiseaux exotiques,* Messiaen film.
Nov 28	*Trois petites Liturgies,* Rome.
Nov 30	*Vingt Regards* and *Visions de l'Amen,* Grenoble.
1974 Jan	Paris, *Poèmes pour Mi* (Felicity Palmer, BBC Symphony Orchestra, Pierre Boulez).

Jan	*Concours International* "Olivier Messiaen" *de composition* in Paris (First Prize winners: Nguyen Thien Dao and Davide Anzaghi).
Jan 15	*Oiseaux exotiques* (Phillipe Entremont) at the Espace Pierre Cardin, Paris.
Jan 16	*Oiseaux exotiques* (Pierre-Laurent Aimard), Paris.
Jan 18	*Oiseaux exotiques* (Pierre-Laurent Aimard, Conductor: Jean-Sebastien Bereau), Paris.
Mar 3	*Oiseaux exotiques* (Michel Beroff; Conductor: Jacques Mercier), Paris.
Mar	Messiaen Week at Karlsruhe (for his 65th birthday): *Méditations* (Almut Rössler) *Messe de la Pentecôte, La Fauvette des jardins* (Yvonne Loriod), first performance in Germany, *Vingt Regards, Couleurs de la Cité Céleste* (Conductor: Oskar Gottfried Blarr, piano solo: Günter Reinhold).

Index